VOYAGES IN ENGLISH
WRITING AND GRAMMAR

How This Practice Book and Assessment Book Answer Key Works	2
Practice Book	**3**
How the Practice Books Work	4
Answers to Chapter 1	5
Answers to Chapter 2	13
Answers to Chapter 3	22
Answers to Chapter 4	30
Answers to Chapter 5	39
Answers to Chapter 6	47
Answers to Chapter 7	56
Answers to Chapter 8	64
Assessment Book	**75**
How the Assessment Books Work	76
Answers to Chapter 1	77
Answers to Chapter 2	81
Answers to Chapter 3	85
Answers to Chapter 4	89
Answers to Chapter 5	93
Answers to Chapter 6	97
Answers to Chapter 7	101
Answers to Chapter 8	105
***Voyages in English* and *Exercises in English* Grammar Correlation Charts**	**113**

Introduction

How This Practice Book and Assessment Book Answer Key Works

For your convenience, each Voyages in English Answer Key is a single but separate volume. This design allows you to grade papers without the need to carry and manage a complete Teacher Guide.

Inside each key you will find the annotated reduced pages from the Practice Book and the Assessment Book for an entire grade level. Two reduced pages appear on a single answer key page. The Practice Book pages, which are accessed more frequently, precede the Assessment Book pages. A description of the Practice Book and how it works follows on page 4. A similar introduction to the Assessment Book is provided on page 76.

Voyages in English and *Exercises in English* Grammar Correlation Charts

Included on pages 113–119 of this Answer Key are correlation charts for anyone who uses both *Voyages in English* and *Exercises in English*. These charts list each grammar section of *Voyages in English* and its corresponding lesson in *Exercises in English*. They provide users with a quick, easy reference to the content in Grades 3–8 for both programs.

VIE Section	EIE Lesson	VIE Section	EIE Lesson	VIE Section	EIE Lesson
Nouns		**Verbals**		**Conjunctions, Interjections**	
1.1	1	5.1	59		
1.2	2	5.2	60–61	9.1	121
1.3	3	5.3	62–63	9.2	122
1.4	4–5	5.4	64–66	9.3	123
1.5	6	5.5	67–68	9.4	124
1.6	7–8	5.6	69–70	9.5	125
Noun		5.7	71–72	9.6	126
Challenge	9	5.8	73	Conjunction,	
		5.9	74	Interjection	
Adjectives		5.10	75	Challenge	127
2.1	10–11	5.11	76–77		
2.2	12	Verbal		**Punctuation and Capitalization**	
2.3	13–14	Challenge	78		
2.4	15	**Adverbs**		10.1	128–132
2.5	16–17	6.1	79	10.2	133–134
Adjective		6.2	80–81	10.3	135
Challenge	18	6.3	82	10.4	136
		6.4	83	10.5	137
Pronouns		6.5	84	Punctuation and	
3.1	19–20	Adverb		Capitalization	
3.2	21–22	Challenge	85	Challenge	138
3.3	22–24				
3.4	25	**Prepositions**		**Diagramming**	
3.5	26	7.1	86	11.1	139
3.6	27–28	7.2	87	11.2	140
3.7	29	7.3	88	11.3	141
3.8	30–33	7.4	89	11.4	142
3.9	33–34	7.5	90	11.5	143
3.10	35	7.6	91	11.6	144
3.11	36	Preposition		11.7	145
Pronoun		Challenge	92	11.8	146
Challenge	37			11.9	147
		Sentences, Phrases, Clauses		11.10	148
Verbs				Diagramming	
4.1	38	8.1	93–101	Challenge	149
4.2	39	8.2	102		
4.3	40	8.3	103–104		
4.4	41	8.4	105		
4.5	42	8.5	106–108		
4.6	43–45	8.6	109		
4.7	46	8.7	110		
4.8	47	8.8	111		
4.9	48	8.9	112		
4.10	49–51	8.10	113–115		
4.11	52–57	8.11	116–119		
Verb		Sentences,			
Challenge	58	Phrases,			
		Clauses			
		Challenge	120		

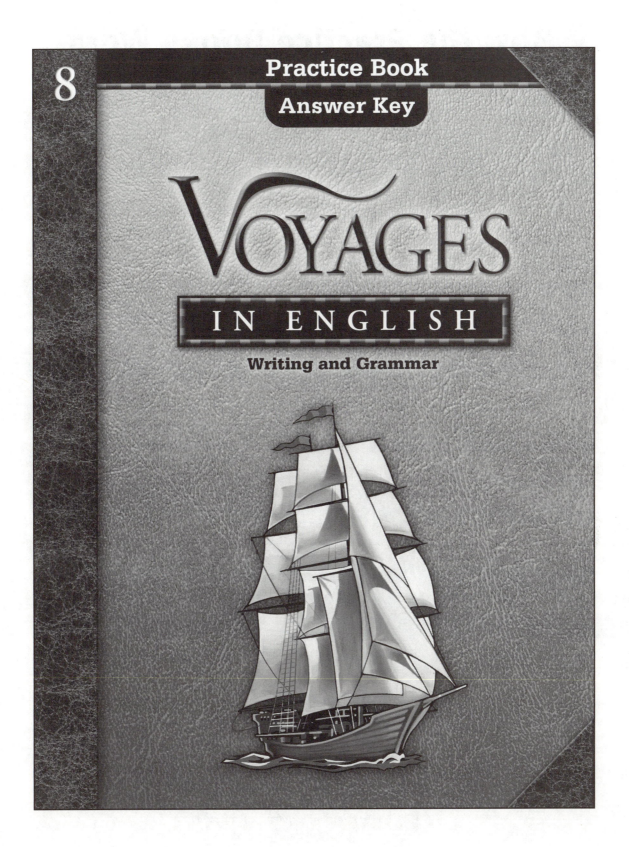

How the Practice Books Work

Fully integrated into the Voyages in English program, the Practice Book pages run parallel with the writing chapters and the grammar sections, providing additional work with the grammar and writing concepts covered in each chapter. Teachers use the Practice Book lessons as student homework and for reteaching and reinforcement, according to the needs of their students.

Every two-day lesson in each of the eight genre chapters of the Voyages Teacher Guide and Student Book is supported by three Practice Book pages—two that reinforce, reassess, or reteach the concepts assessed in the daily Focus on Grammar quiz and one that reinforces the characteristics of the genre or the skills taught in the lesson. These three Practice Book pages are clearly labeled to show how they correlate to the writing chapter or the parallel grammar section that is part of the integrated study. The Self-Assessment at the end of every chapter allows students to evaluate how well they mastered the writing and grammar content.

The Practice Book offers 17 pages of rigorous reinforcement per student book chapter: 2 genre lessons, 3 skills lessons, 11 grammar lessons, and a self-assessment writing and grammar rubric.

Practice Book Rubrics

Each Practice Book page offers reinforcement for students who had trouble mastering the lessons' writing and grammar skills.

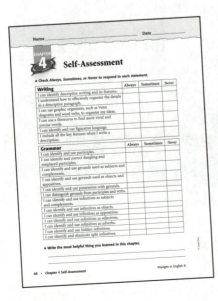

An additional student self-assessment tool, found in the Practice Book, allows young writers to see how well they have mastered the chapter content.

4 • Voyages in English

CHAPTER 1 — Singular and Plural Nouns

- Underline the singular noun in each sentence. Then write the plural form of the noun. Use a dictionary if necessary.

1. She was sworn in after reciting an <u>oath</u>. _____ **oaths**
2. The <u>moose</u> ran faster than I imagined it could. _____ **moose**
3. I like studying at the <u>library</u>. _____ **libraries**
4. The <u>woman</u> next door is kind and generous. _____ **women**
5. I noticed that one <u>antenna</u> was missing. _____ **antennae**
6. He saw a <u>mouse</u> scampering between the boxes. _____ **mice**
7. The caravan stopped at an <u>oasis</u>. _____ **oases**
8. Each <u>hoof</u> needed to be cleaned. _____ **hooves**
9. I watched as the huge <u>bear</u> slept. _____ **bears**
10. Did you see that beautiful red <u>fox</u>? _____ **foxes**
11. She showed us the delicate antique <u>tray</u>. _____ **trays**

CHAPTER 1 — More Singular and Plural Nouns

- Underline the singular noun in each sentence. Then go back and circle the first letter of each plural noun. Write the letters in order on the lines below to find the answer to the riddle.

1. Ten (m)onkeys swung from the <u>vine</u>.
2. I heard faint (e)choes coming from the <u>cave</u>.
3. We are (a)lumni of the same <u>school</u>.
4. The (s)helves in the <u>kitchen</u> need to be rearranged.
5. He rides (u)nicycles in the <u>circus</u>.
6. She uses home (r)emedies to treat a <u>cold</u>.
7. How many (e)xits are in this <u>building</u>?
8. Five (m)oose stepped into the <u>clearing</u>.
9. He has three (e)ights in his card <u>hand</u>.
10. How many (n)uclei are in a single <u>cell</u>?
11. Grace caught six (t)rout.

What is an inchworm's favorite math skill?
Answer: <u>m</u> <u>e</u> <u>a</u> <u>s</u> <u>u</u> <u>r</u> <u>e</u> <u>m</u> <u>e</u> <u>n</u> <u>t</u>
          1 2 3 4 5 6 7 8 9 10 11

Now use your answer in a sentence.
Sentences will vary.

Practice Book Answers • 5

Name _____ Date _____

CHAPTER 1
Nouns as Subjects and Subject Complements

- Circle the letter under *Subject* if the underlined noun is the subject of the sentence. Circle the letter under *Complement* if the underlined noun renames the subject. Write the circled letters in order on the lines below. If your answers are correct, the answer to the riddle will be revealed.

	Subject	Complement
1. Ms. Hernandez is our new science <u>teacher</u>.	A	(S)
2. <u>Jesse</u> bought a new jacket with his allowance.	(W)	O
3. The <u>sun</u> is rising over the mountain.	(I)	R
4. Jazzy was my mom's big tiger-striped <u>cat</u>.	E	(N)
5. The white <u>rabbit</u> scrambled under the fence.	(E)	T
6. Lisa's <u>bicycle</u> got a flat tire on the way to school.	(W)	L
7. Gina and Chantel were the most talented <u>dancers</u> I knew.	A	(H)
8. She became my <u>friend</u> at summer camp.	O	(I)
9. My <u>brother</u> used to play professional tennis.	(N)	M
10. Maya remained the <u>president</u> of the computer company.	H	(E)

What do you call a pig's complaint?

Answer: <u>s</u> <u>w</u> <u>i</u> <u>n</u> <u>e</u> <u>w</u> <u>h</u> <u>i</u> <u>n</u> <u>e</u>
        1 2 3 4 5 6 7 8 9 10

Name _____ Date _____

CHAPTER 1
What Makes a Good Personal Narrative?

- Read the personal narrative. Then answer the questions.

> I could hardly believe it. Every step and every move was perfect! I had spent six long months learning the routine. It seemed every time I performed the dance in rehearsal, I had made a mistake. Once I forgot my dance shoes. But this time, with the spotlight shining brightly on me, blinding my eyes to the audience and tingling my skin, I felt myself dancing as if I were in a dream. The music flowed through my veins like blood, the pounding of the drums keeping time with the pounding of my heart. I wasn't just dancing to the music, I was the music.

1. What would be the best title for this personal narrative—"Dance Rehearsal" or "Dancing a Dream?"
   Dancing a Dream
   Why do you think so?
   Answers will vary.

2. Who do you think is the intended audience for this narrative?
   Why do you think so?
   Answers will vary.

3. What reaction do you think the author wants from the reader? What kind of feelings and emotions is he or she trying to invoke?
   Answers will vary.

4. The author included one irrelevant detail. What is it?
   Once I forgot my dance shoes.

5. This narrative is told in chronological order. What words did the author use to provide coherence?
   Possible answers: six long months, every time, this time

CHAPTER 1

Introduction, Body, and Conclusion

- A personal narrative includes an introduction, a body, and a conclusion. Write *I*, *B*, or *C* to show whether each of the following sentences would most likely come in the introduction, body, or conclusion of a personal narrative. **Accept any answer students can justify.**

1. **C** I sat back and closed my eyes; it was finally over.
2. **C** Little did I know that I would never again return to Thor Mountain.
3. **I** When I woke up that morning, it seemed like any other day.
4. **B** We ran as fast as we could as the bear followed close behind.
5. **B** The wind howled like a wild animal outside my window.
6. **I** I don't like to tell secrets, but this one was too good to keep to myself!

- Choose a personal narrative topic from the list. Write an engaging introduction for a personal narrative about the topic.

winning a championship game	death of a grandparent
a summer adventure	moving to another city
finding a lost pet	

Answers will vary.

- Plan the rest of your narrative by completing a Word/Idea Web like the one on page 137. Draw your web on a separate sheet of paper.

6 • Lesson 2
Voyages in English 8

CHAPTER 1

Nouns as Objects and Object Complements

- Circle the noun used as an indirect object in each sentence. Count the letters in each answer and write the number in the box.

1. Manny gave his (dog) a treat for performing the trick. [3]
2. The community center offers (people) a variety of classes. [6]
3. Jon sent (Maria) an invitation to the winter dance. [5]
4. Did Krista give the (aerialist) the award? [9]
5. The postal worker brought the (manager) a package. [7]

- Circle the term used as an object complement in each sentence. Count the letters in each answer and write the number in the box.

6. We named our new pet snake (Bowe). [4]
7. Kyra decided to appoint Elena club (secretary). [9]
8. Sergio and Jake considered the coaches their (friends). [7]
9. The girls chose Cherise ("Miss Congeniality.") [16]
10. The critics called the new show a (disaster). [8]

- Now crack the code. Use the key below to write the letter for each number on the lines below. If your answers are correct, you'll answer the riddle.

Who always hurries but is never late?

Answer: <u>J u s t i n   T i m e</u>
       3 6 5 9 7 4   9 7 16 8

3 = J   4 = N   5 = S   6 = U   7 = I   8 = E   9 = T   16 = M

Voyages in English 8
Section 1.4 • 5

Practice Book Answers • 7

CHAPTER 1 Possessive Nouns

- **Rewrite each sentence so that the appropriate noun shows possession. The first one is done for you.**

1. The reports written by Min and Juvia were excellent.
   Min's and Juvia's reports were excellent.
2. The father of McKenzie and Trent is a famous writer.
   McKenzie and Trent's father is a famous writer.
3. The tree house belonging to the boys is over the stream.
   The boys' tree house is over the stream.
4. The most familiar story written by Charles Dickens is about a boy named Pip.
   Charles Dickens's most familiar story is about a boy named Pip.
5. These old books belonging to my father-in-law are priceless.
   My father-in-law's old books are priceless.
6. Tham borrowed the bike owned by her best friend.
   Tham borrowed her best friend's bike.
7. The toys belonging to the children were scattered across the floor.
   The children's toys were scattered across the floor.
8. The pie made by Ben and Theo won first prize at the fair.
   Ben and Theo's pie won first prize at the fair.
9. The purse belonging to that woman was stolen at the park.
   That woman's purse was stolen at the park.
10. Manners should be the priority of every gentleman.
    Manners should be every gentleman's priority.

CHAPTER 1 Appositives

- **Circle each noun used as an appositive and underline the noun it explains.**

1. Corey, my little (brother), is the noisiest person I've ever met.
2. Jill loves potatoes, the tastiest (vegetable) in the world—or so she claims.
3. We should contact Mr. Sanchez, Miguel's (coach), for a meeting.
4. Wendy traveled to London, the (capital) of England, to visit her pen pal.
5. The penguin, a flightless (bird), lives near the South Pole.
6. My sister, (Maggie), makes the best cookies.
7. Dr. Fredricks, a college (professor), will speak to our class tomorrow.
8. The novel (Holes) won a Newbery Medal.

- **Write four sentences that use a noun as an appositive.**

9. Sentences will vary.
10. Sentences will vary.
11. Sentences will vary.
12. Sentences will vary.

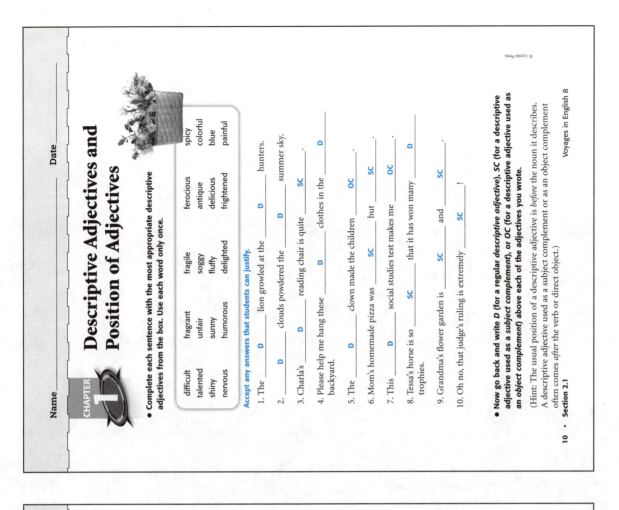

CHAPTER 1 Varied Sentences

- Identify each type of sentence by circling S (simple), CD (compound), or CX (complex). Then, for each compound or complex sentence you find, separate it into the two or more sentences that were combined. Write these simple sentences on the lines, adding or deleting words as needed.

1. Lin wanted spaghetti for dinner, but Tom wanted hamburgers.   S (CD) CX
   Sentences may vary. Sample answer: Lin wanted spaghetti for dinner.
   Tom wanted hamburgers for dinner.

2. Baseball, soccer, and tennis are Terrance's favorite sports.   (S) CD CX

3. Brandon, Joe's little brother, was the funniest person in the class.   (S) CD CX

4. The cat ran under the fence, and the dog followed in hot pursuit.   S (CD) CX

5. Jessica loves visiting her cousins because they live on a big farm.   S CD (CX)

6. Though he is behind in his math homework, Bryan is ahead in English.   S CD (CX)

CHAPTER 1 Demonstrative, Interrogative, and Indefinite Adjectives

- Underline the demonstrative or interrogative adjective in each sentence. Write D if the adjective is demonstrative and I if it is interrogative.

1. Those flowers belong to my sister.   D
2. Which backpack is yours?   I
3. What name did you give the puppy?   I
4. That painting took me four days to complete.   D
5. Which road did you decide to take?   I
6. He asked, "What museums do you want to visit?"   I
7. Did you wear this dress for the wedding?   D
8. These boys won't let us play baseball with them.   D
9. Which video game do you want to buy?   I
10. I found the stray kittens in this garage.   D

- Complete each sentence with an indefinite adjective from the box. Use each word only once. Then go back to check whether any other words from the box would also fit. Write that word on the line after the sentence. If no other word fits, write NO.

| any | all | another | both | few |
| many | much | several | some | such |

11. _____ vegetables are tastier than others.
12. There are _____ shoes to choose from.
13. How _____ money did you bring?
14. I did not see _____ deer in the woods that day.   No
15. Here is _____ test for you to grade.
16. There are too _____ students in the class.   No
17. May I have a _____ coins for the meter?   No
18. I like to taste _____ chocolate.

Accept all correct answers: 11. Many, Several, Some, Few; 12. many, several, some, few; 13. much; 14. many, another, several, both, some, few; 15. another; 16. many, few; 17. few; 18. any, all, much, some

CHAPTER 1

Comparative and Superlative Adjectives

- Read each sentence. Check to see if the comparative or superlative adjective is used correctly. If it is used correctly, write C on the line. If it is not used correctly, write the correct comparative or superlative adjective on the line.

1. Theresa's (hair) is *much longer* than Sara's. _____ C
2. Emilio is the *more smarter* (person) in my class. _____ smartest
3. My aunt is the *most intelligent* (woman) I know. _____ C
4. Carrie shared her *deepest* (secrets) with me. _____ C
5. The cheetah is one of the *most fastest* (animals) on earth. _____ fastest
6. Casanova is *prettier* than my other cats. _____ C
7. Is that the *highest* (mountain) you've ever climbed? _____ C
8. Jenny's (eyes) are *darkest* than mine. _____ darker
9. Shane is *more taller* than Jared this year. _____ taller
10. Mr. Grant was the *more interesting* (speaker) of them all. _____ most interesting

- Now go back and read each sentence again. Circle the noun each adjective modifies.

- Write three of your own sentences, comparing these nouns:

A. two foods
   Sentences will vary.

B. three friends
   Sentences will vary.

C. two sports
   Sentences will vary.

Section 2.3 • 13

CHAPTER 1

Few and *Little* with Count and Noncount Nouns

- Write the correct adjective—*few, fewer, fewest, little, less,* or *least*—to complete each sentence. Circle the letter under *Count* if the adjective modifies a count noun. Circle the letter under *Noncount* if the adjective modifies a noncount noun.

		Count	Noncount
1. There is __less__ corn on his plate than mine.	W	(S)
2. Justin had the __least__ money of anyone in the group.	I	(T)
3. We coached __fewer__ players this year than last.	(E)	R
4. There are only a __few__ minutes left in the hour.	(P)	C
5. Make sure to give this puppy a __little__ love every day.	A	(O)
6. We have only a __few__ books on the shelves in the corner.	(N)	M
7. My garden produced __fewer__ flowers than expected.	(N)	U
8. Will you put a __little__ mustard on my hot dog?	H	(O)
9. Nathan has constructed the __fewest__ model cars.	(P)	L
10. There are __few__ brownies left at the bake sale.	(E)	A
11. Of all subjects, I have the __least__ (knowledge) in biology.	R	(T)
12. There is __little__ (peace) left in that part of the world.	E	(S)

- Now go back and circle three abstract nouns.

- Read the circled letters in order, from top to bottom and bottom to top. Then write the letters on the lines below.

Answer: <u>s</u> <u>t</u> <u>e</u> <u>p</u> <u>o</u> <u>n</u> <u>n</u> <u>o</u> <u>p</u> <u>e</u> <u>t</u> <u>s</u>
         1 2 3 4 5 6 7 8 9 10 11 12

What do you notice about these letters?
They form a *palindrome*, an expression whose letters read the same forward and backward.

14 • Section 2.4

Name _____ Date _____

CHAPTER 1

Exact Words

- Write specific, interesting adjectives, verbs, or adverbs to complete each sentence. Avoid overused words such as *big, very, nice, pretty, good, great,* and *bad.*

  1. We _____ over the _____ bridge before the hunters could catch us.
  2. Josh became _____ impatient with his little brother Jake.
  3. Bring in the horses before that _____ fire can _____ the wheat field!
  4. Tara giggled _____ as all eyes _____ at her, waiting for her speech.

  Answers will vary. Make sure words are specific and interesting as well as relevant in the context of the sentence.

- The verb *said* is one of the most overused words in the English language. Underline the word used in place of *said* in each sentence. Then find and circle these six words in the word search below. Words can go across, up, down, and diagonal.

  "I just don't know," Mom sighed.   Lisa shouted, "Don't open that door!"
  "How are you?" Jason inquired shyly.   "Please bring in the trash," Dad pleaded.
  "That painting is beautiful," he whispered.   "That is hilarious!" she laughed.

  ```
  S X G L W G B C M L I O G N
  A I W D F H G J K A L M O E
  Z N N H S K I V C U M N L D
  S Q A I O U D S L G A B E E
  V U F B C P U T P H F G E T
  S I G H E D G E Y E T R S U
  O R E P L E A D E D R G N O
  P E M K L K S X E C V E M H
  N D Y E H I J H G M B I D S
  ```

Name _____ Date _____

CHAPTER 1

Adjective Phrases and Clauses

- Draw a line from each subject in the first column to the item in the second column that creates the best complete sentence. Then underline each adjective phrase or clause. Write *AP* on the line if it is an adjective phrase and *AC* if it is an adjective clause.

  AP 1. The tiger   on freeways drive too fast.
  AC 2. The cruise ship   who is willing to practice may make the pros.
  AC 3. Rivers   in the brush has golden eyes.
  AP 4. The girl   which is in the harbor, is going to Mexico.
  AP 5. Some people   who never learn to apologize.
  AC 6. Parrots   with the button eyes is old and worn.
  AP 7. Italy   that provide drinking water are plentiful.
  AC 8. An athlete   is a country with many famous tourist attractions.
  AP 9. The teddy bear   with red hair gave me a valentine.
  AC 10. Sorry are those   that can learn to talk cost a lot of money.

CHAPTER 1 Self-Assessment

- Check *Always*, *Sometimes*, or *Never* to respond to each statement.

Writing

	Always	Sometimes	Never
I can identify a personal narrative and its features.			
I understand how to write an effective introduction, body, and conclusion for a personal narrative.			
I can use a time line to organize my ideas.			
I use a variety of sentences (simple, compound, and complex) in my writing.			
I use specific, interesting words in my writing.			
I include all the key features in a personal narrative.			

Grammar

	Always	Sometimes	Never
I can identify and use singular and plural nouns.			
I can identify and use nouns as subjects and subject complements.			
I can identify and use nouns as objects and object complements.			
I can identify and use appositives.			
I can identify nouns used to show singular and plural possession and use them correctly.			
I can identify nouns used to show joint possession and use them correctly.			
I can identify and use descriptive adjectives and determine when they are used as subject complements and object complements.			
I can identify and use demonstrative, interrogative, and indefinite adjectives.			
I can identify and use comparative and superlative adjectives.			
I can identify and use *few* and *little* with count and noncount nouns.			
I can identify and use adjective phrases and adjective clauses.			

- What was the most helpful thing you learned in this chapter?

CHAPTER 2 Person, Number, and Gender of Pronouns

- Underline the pronoun in each sentence. Write the pronoun's person (*first, second, third*) and number (*singular, plural*). Then identify the gender (*masculine, feminine, neuter*) of all third person singular pronouns or place an X when gender doesn't apply. The first one is done for you.

	Person	Number	Gender
1. Mina and I shared an ice-cream sundae.	first	singular	X
2. Josh, did you call last night?	second	singular	X
3. The lawn mower belongs to them.	third	plural	X
4. Kylie handed him the first-place trophy.	third	singular	masculine
5. The house we want to buy is far away.	first	plural	X
6. She is Katie's best friend.	third	singular	feminine
7. The dog was thirsty, so Vinh gave it water.	third	singular	neuter
8. Does the teacher have tickets for us?	first	plural	X
9. They will bring potato salad to the picnic.	third	plural	X
10. Jack gave her a kitten for Christmas.	third	singular	feminine

Name _____ Date _____

CHAPTER 2 — Subject Pronouns

- **Circle the subject pronoun that correctly completes each sentence.**

1. The ones who won first place were Mia and (**I**, me).
2. Jerri and (**she**, her) are the only ones who like peas.
3. It was (**we**, us) who brought the chocolate cake.
4. The lionesses lying under the tree are Sheba and (her, **she**).
5. (Them, **They**) are both successful lawyers.
6. (Him, **He**) and Booker both hit home runs in the game.
7. Did (it, **you**) know that cats walk on their toes?
8. Theo, did (**you**, your) remember to lock the door?
9. Darius is talented, but (him, **he**) still needs lots of practice.
10. The people who moved in next door were (**they**, them).

- **Now go back and underline the first letter of each answer. Use the key below to decode the letters you underlined. Write the letters, in order to fill in the boxes. If your answers are correct, you will have a palindrome (a word or sentence that reads the same forward and backward) that answers this question:**

What is zero, no matter what?

I = N   T = R   H = O   W = V   S = E   Y = D
E = N   V = E   R = O   O = D   D = D

1.	2.	3.	4.	5.	6.	7.	8.
N	E	V	E	R	O	D	D

9.	10.
O	R

E	V	E	N

Palindrome: never odd or even

Name _____ Date _____

CHAPTER 2 — What Makes a Good How-to Article?

- **A good how-to article includes concise, logically ordered steps. Read the how-to paragraph. Delete three unnecessary or illogical sentences. Then circle six transition words that help the reader know the order of the steps.**

Fluffy, Shake!

Most people think a cat cannot be trained, but they are wrong. Cats are intelligent creatures that are highly responsive to suggestion, just as dogs are. ~~Most people are cat-lovers.~~ (First), decide on a behavior that you'd like your cat to learn, such as shaking your hand. ~~Dogs are also easily trained.~~ (Second), make sure you have plenty of treats ready to reinforce your cat's behavior. (Begin) by placing the treat in the center of your hand where your cat can't see it. (Next), reach down and wait for your cat to reach for the food with its paw. (Then) as your cat reaches up, say firmly, "Shake." Give your cat the treat if it performs correctly. You want your cat to associate your extended hand and the word *shake* with a tasty treat. ~~You can find cat treats and toys in your local pet store.~~ Repeat this step several times. (Finally), try it without the treat. Your cat should reach up to see if there is something tasty in your hand. Keep practicing, and believe it or not, you can train your cat!

- **Answer the following questions about this how-to paragraph.**

1. Who would be the best audience for this how-to paragraph? Why?
   Possible answer
   any cat owner, because the language is simple and casual rather than scientific or technical

2. What is the first step in training your cat to perform a trick?
   Decide on the behavior you'd like your cat to learn.

3. What is the last step?
   Say "shake" without giving your cat the treat.

4. What is the conclusion of this paragraph? What does it promise or predict?
   If you keep practicing, you can train your cat

5. Write another introductory sentence for this paragraph. Remember that the introduction should grab the reader's attention and tell what the paragraph is about.
   Answers will vary.

Name _____ Date _____

CHAPTER 2 — Object Pronouns

• Underline the object pronoun in each sentence. Then tell how the pronoun is used by crossing out the letter in the corresponding column.

	Direct Object	Indirect Object	Object of a Prep.
1. The next class production was chosen by Leah and <u>me</u>.	G	O	~~R~~
2. We chose Shakespeare, who gave <u>us</u> beautiful words.	O	~~T~~	D
3. I've heard many fascinating stories about <u>him</u>.	G	R	~~T~~
4. Thirty-seven full-length plays were written by <u>him</u>.	A	M	H
5. The theater-going crowds of England loved <u>him</u>.	~~S~~	M	A
6. Shakespeare wrote plays about love, history, and tragedy for <u>them</u>.	R	M	~~E~~
7. Shakespeare was married to Anne Hathaway, but he did not take <u>her</u> to London.	~~O~~	E	A
8. Queen Elizabeth supported the arts, and Shakespeare performed for <u>her</u> several times.	N	S	~~E~~
9. His theater, the Globe, was closed in 1642, but art patrons rebuilt <u>it</u> in 1995.	W	G	O
10. Shakespeare liked to entertain people, and he delighted <u>them</u> with puns and comic characters.	~~T~~	O	D

• Now write the leftover letters in order from left to right on the lines below to spell out a sentence.

Answer: <u>G</u> <u>o</u> <u>o</u> <u>d</u> <u>g</u> <u>r</u> <u>a</u> <u>m</u> <u>m</u> <u>a</u> <u>r</u>
        1   2   3   4   5   6

<u>m</u> <u>e</u> <u>a</u> <u>n</u> <u>s</u> <u>g</u> <u>o</u> <u>o</u> <u>d</u> <u>g</u> <u>r</u> <u>a</u> <u>d</u> <u>e</u> <u>s</u> .
 6 7   7 8   9 10 10

Name _____ Date _____

CHAPTER 2 — Pronouns after *Than* or *As*

• Replace the underlined word or words with the correct pronoun in each sentence. Then write any words that are missing but understood. The first one is done for you.

	Pronoun	Missing Words
1. Troy is much more athletic than <u>Michael</u>.	he	is athletic
2. Those students performed as well as <u>these students</u>.	they	performed
3. Our baseball team won more games than <u>the Tigers</u>.	they	won
4. I like chocolate cake more than <u>Jerome</u>.	he	likes chocolate cake
5. Marcus ran no farther than <u>our team</u>.	we	ran
6. Jordan plays racquetball as well as <u>Lauren</u>.	she	plays racquetball
7. I'm sure that I can dance as well as <u>Ms. Thompson</u>.	she	can dance
8. The fifth-hour class thinks that it will raise more money than <u>our class</u>.	we	will raise

• Write the four letters that appear in the pronouns you wrote to spell a direction.

Answer: <u>w</u> <u>e</u> <u>s</u> <u>t</u>

• Now use those four letters to solve this riddle with two nearly rhyming words.

What do you call loving bird sounds?

Answer: <u>s</u> <u>w</u> <u>e</u> <u>e</u> <u>t</u> <u>t</u> <u>w</u> <u>e</u> <u>e</u> <u>t</u> <u>s</u>

CHAPTER 2

Making Instructions Clear and Concise

- One way to make instructions clear and concise is to have good organization. The steps should come in chronological order (1–9). Number in the correct order these steps for making French toast.

  A. __6__ Place bread slices in the hot pan or on the griddle.
  B. __5__ Turn over the bread in the mixture so that both sides are coated.
  C. __9__ Cover your French toast with butter, syrup, powdered sugar, fresh berries, whipped cream, or other toppings of your choice. Eat!
  D. __3__ In a bowl beat together two eggs, 1/4 tsp. vanilla, 1/8 cup milk, and a dash of salt.
  E. __8__ When the second side is done, place the toast on a serving plate.
  F. __1__ Gather the ingredients.
  G. __2__ Let butter melt in a large frying pan or on a griddle while you mix the ingredients.
  H. __4__ Place the bread in the egg mixture.
  I. __7__ Flip bread over after the first side is golden brown.

- On a separate piece of paper, list the steps for making one of your favorite dishes. Number your steps in chronological order.

CHAPTER 2

Possessive Pronouns and Adjectives

- Rewrite each sentence with a correct possessive pronoun or adjective.

  1. Our has lemon trees.
     Ours has lemon trees.
  2. I think that backpack is your's.
     I think that backpack is yours.
  3. My is the best of the bunch.
     Mine is the best of the bunch.
  4. Her will crack if you are not careful.
     Hers will crack if you are not careful.
  5. There snow blower broke yesterday.
     Their snow blower broke yesterday.
  6. My requires extra maintenance.
     Mine requires extra maintenance.
  7. His' painting was too beautiful to describe.
     His painting was too beautiful to describe.
  8. Hours is painted yellow.
     Ours is painted yellow.
  9. His's seems sluggish.
     His seems sluggish.
  10. They'res are floating on the pond.
      Theirs are floating on the pond.

- Use the following possessive pronoun in an original sentence.

  11. mine
      Sample answer: Mine came from India.

Name _____ Date _____

CHAPTER 2 — Intensive and Reflexive Pronouns

- **Complete each sentence with the correct intensive or reflexive pronoun. Identify each pronoun by circling *I* for intensive or *R* for reflexive.**

		Intensive	Reflexive
1. You may all find **yourselves** lost without a map.		I	**(R)**
2. Maria must give **herself** time to study.		I	**(R)**
3. I **myself** am unable to attend the wedding.		**(I)**	R
4. You can teach the class **yourself**.		**(I)**	R
5. He **himself** ran the marathon.		**(I)**	R
6. We allowed **ourselves** to enjoy the scenery.		I	**(R)**
7. They will plant new trees **themselves**.		**(I)**	R
8. The horse **itself** could win the race.		**(I)**	R

- **Use each pronoun in a sentence.**

9. itself **Answers will vary.**
10. themselves **Answers will vary.**
11. yourself **Answers will vary.**
12. herself **Answers will vary.**
13. ourselves **Answers will vary.**
14. himself **Answers will vary.**

Voyages in English 8 — Section 3.6 • 25

Name _____ Date _____

CHAPTER 2 — Revising Sentences

- **Rewrite each of the following rambling or run-on sentences as two or more separate sentences. Take out any unnecessary words.**

1. If you want to learn how to cook, you should begin by buying the proper cookware, including pots, pans, and a grill, as well as utensils like spoons, ladles, and spatulas and also have a pantry full of lots of dried herbs and spices to add fresh, exciting flavors to your foods.
   Sample answer: If you like to cook, you should begin by buying the proper cookware and utensils, including pots, pans, a grill, spoons, ladles, and spatulas. You should also have a pantry full of dried herbs and spices to add fresh, exciting flavors to your foods.

2. Some people prefer grilling outside to cooking indoors, grilling is an entire and complete art of its own that takes much skill and lots of practice.
   Answers will vary.

3. You can attend one of several famous cooking schools that are in existence around the world, many of them specialize in different kinds of foods as well as restaurant management.
   Answers will vary.

4. Vegetarians eat only breads, fruits, vegetables, and also sometimes they eat fish, most people like meat way, way too much to ever give it up for good.
   Answers will vary.

26 • Lesson 3 — Voyages in English 8

CHAPTER 2: Interrogative Pronouns and Demonstrative Pronouns

- Write the correct interrogative or demonstrative pronoun to complete each grammar rule. **Accept any answers students can justify.**

what	whom	whose	this	who
these	those	that	which	

This interrogative pronoun . . .

1. refers to persons. It is often the subject in a question. __who__
2. refers to persons. It is the object of a verb. __whom__
3. is used when asking about possession. __whose__
4. is used when asking about a group or class. __which__
5. refers to persons. It is the object of a preposition. __whom__
6. is used for asking about things. __what__
7. is used for seeking information. __what__

This demonstrative pronoun . . .

8. points out something singular that is near. __this__
9. points out something plural that is near. __these__
10. points out something singular that is distant. __that__
11. points out something plural that is distant. __those__

CHAPTER 2: Agreement of Pronouns and Antecedents

- Rewrite each sentence to correct the pronoun to make it agree with the underlined antecedent.

1. <u>Devon and Jared</u> were late to class, but he will make up the time at break.
   __Devon and Jared were late to class, but they will make up the time at break.__
2. Alicia's friend <u>Sue</u> is back from Italy, and they have many interesting stories to tell.
   __Alicia's friend Sue is back from Italy, and she has many interesting stories to tell.__
3. <u>Troy</u> is the best athlete I know, but it doesn't want to try out for any teams.
   __Troy is the best athlete I know, but he doesn't want to try out for any teams.__
4. I don't know why those <u>stories</u> were deleted, because I think it was good.
   __I don't know why those stories were deleted, because I think they were good.__
5. <u>Rachel and Stella</u> gave a great presentation, but, unfortunately, we forgot the slides.
   __Rachel and Stella gave a great presentation, but, unfortunately, they forgot the slides.__
6. Our prize <u>poodle</u> won Most Talented, but they failed to win first prize.
   __Our prize poodle won Most Talented, but it failed to win first prize.__
7. We wanted to invite <u>Ms. Washington</u>, but we didn't know how to contact them.
   __We wanted to invite Ms. Washington, but we didn't know how to contact her.__
8. The <u>mailbox</u> is next to the driveway; don't forget to check her every night.
   __The mailbox is next to the driveway; don't forget to check it every night.__

- Use each pronoun in a compound sentence. Be sure each pronoun has an antecedent with which it agrees.

9. he __Sample answer: Jake is my friend, but he is on vacation.__
10. she __Answers will vary.__
11. it __Answers will vary.__

CHAPTER 2 — Roots

- Study the roots in the box below. Then complete each sentence with a word based on your knowledge of these roots. (Hint: You will not use all the roots.)

vac = empty	phys = body	terra = earth
chrono = time	tox = poison	vis = see
arch = old	hydro = water	meter = measure
script = write	neg = no	tempo = time
	bio = life	
	civ = citizen	
	grat = pleasing	
	brev = short	

1. **Archaeology** is the study of ancient ruins and fossils.
2. A **biologist** studies living things.
3. Any poisonous substance is said to be **toxic**.
4. Any person who sees well has good **vision**.
5. We use a **thermometer** to measure temperature.
6. An unoccupied apartment is **vacant**.
7. A book is a written **manuscript** before it is published.
8. Instead of saying "no," a robot might say, "**negative**."
9. To thank someone for a kind act is to show **gratitude**.
10. An **abbreviation** is a shortened form of a word.

Lesson 4 • 29

CHAPTER 2 — Relative Pronouns

- Underline the relative pronoun in each sentence. List each antecedent in the column at the right.

Antecedent

1. The yams <u>that</u> we ate with dinner gave me a stomachache. — **yams**
2. The electric oven, <u>which</u> was bought last week, is broken. — **oven**
3. *Ulysses*, <u>which</u> is a well-known book, can be challenging to read. — **Ulysses**
4. Ryan, <u>who</u> works at the animal shelter, is planning to be a veterinarian. — **Ryan**
5. The lifelong friends <u>whose</u> craft store this is made this quilt. — **friends**
6. Megan asked Olivia, <u>whom</u> she greatly admired, to be a mentor. — **Olivia**
7. The oranges <u>that</u> we picked made a jug of delicious orange juice. — **oranges**
8. Tia and Sara, <u>who</u> were prima ballerinas, own a dance studio. — **Tia and Sara**
9. The snow, <u>which</u> came down all night, covered our cars. — **snow**
10. Trains that pass by our house have very loud whistles. — **Trains**
11. Is this the elephant <u>that</u> can do all the funny tricks? — **elephant**
12. The people <u>who</u> were cast in *Our Town* know a lot about Thornton Wilder. — **people**
13. The sonnet <u>that</u> was read aloud reflected Shakespeare's style. — **sonnet**

- Now enter the first letter of each antecedent on the corresponding line below. If your answers are correct, you will reveal the answer to this riddle.

The more of them you take, the more you leave behind. What are they?

Answer: <u>y</u> <u>o</u> <u>u</u> <u>r</u> <u>f</u> <u>o</u> <u>o</u> <u>t</u> <u>s</u> <u>t</u> <u>e</u> <u>p</u> <u>s</u>
 1 2 3 4   5 6 7 8 9 10 11 12 13

30 • Section 3.9

Name _____ Date _____

CHAPTER 2: Indefinite Pronouns

- Circle the indefinite pronoun in each sentence.

1. (Much) of what we know about our universe comes from the telescope.
2. Long ago (nobody) believed that Earth revolved around the sun.
3. (Someone) had to invent an instrument that allowed people to see the planets up close.
4. The planets revolve around the sun, (each) at its own speed.
5. (Everything) in the heavens looks closer than it actually is.
6. When a star dies, (another) will likely take its place.
7. There is (something) exciting and mysterious about space.
8. Thanks to Galileo, (everybody) knows that the sun is the center of our universe.
9. Is there (anyone) in the world who is not fascinated by stargazing?
10. To me, (nothing) sounds more exciting than riding in a spaceship.
11. Among my friends, (few) think humans will eventually live on the moon.
12. (Some) in the scientific community believe that there was once life on Mars.

Section 3.10 • 31

Name _____ Date _____

CHAPTER 2: Dictionary

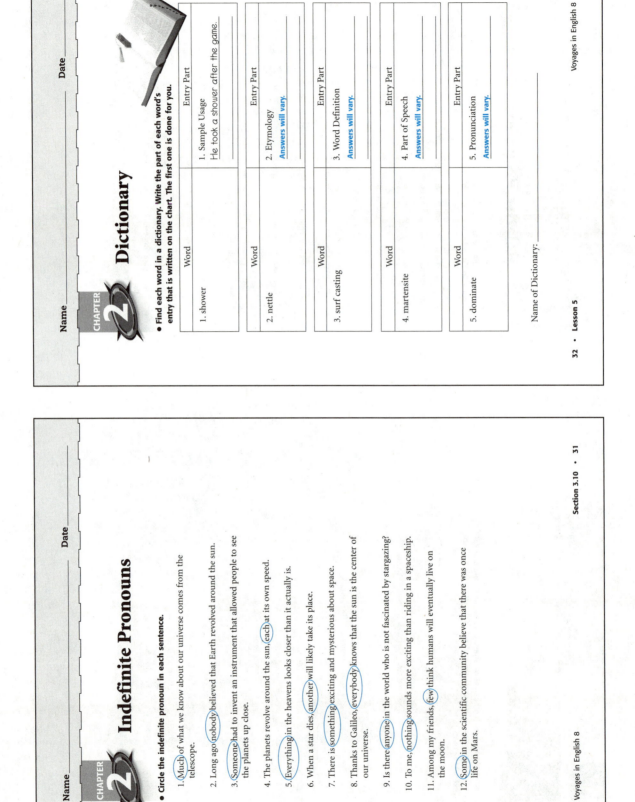

- Find each word in a dictionary. Write the part of each word's entry that is written on the chart. The first one is done for you.

Word	Entry Part
1. shower	1. Sample Usage He took a shower after the game.
2. nettle	2. Etymology **Answers will vary.**
3. surf casting	3. Word Definition **Answers will vary.**
4. martensite	4. Part of Speech **Answers will vary.**
5. dominate	5. Pronunciation **Answers will vary.**

Name of Dictionary: _____

32 • Lesson 5

CHAPTER 2

Self-Assessment

- Check *Always*, *Sometimes*, or *Never* to respond to each statement.

Writing

	Always	Sometimes	Never
I can identify a how-to article and its features.			
I can write clear, concise steps in logical order, provide appropriate details, and omit unnecessary information.			
I can trim rambling or run-on sentences, making every word count.			
I can identify roots and use them to understand the meaning of words.			
I can identify and use all the parts of a dictionary entry.			
I can include all the key features when I write a how-to article.			

Grammar

	Always	Sometimes	Never
I can identify and use the correct pronoun to show person, number, and gender.			
I can identify and use subject pronouns.			
I can identify and use object pronouns.			
I can choose the correct pronoun to use after *than* and *as*.			
I can identify and use possessive pronouns.			
I can identify and use intensive and reflexive pronouns.			
I can show agreement between pronouns and their antecedents.			
I can identify and use interrogative and demonstrative pronouns.			
I can identify and use relative pronouns.			
I can identify and use indefinite pronouns.			
I can show agreement between indefinite pronouns and verbs.			

- Write the most useful thing you learned in this chapter.

_____

CHAPTER 2

Agreement with Indefinite Pronouns

- Underline the indefinite pronoun and circle the verb in each sentence. If the verb is correct, write *correct* on the line. If the verb is incorrect, write the correct verb on the line.

1. <u>Some</u> (offers) educational programs on whales. __offer__
2. <u>Nobody</u> from the three groups (want) to miss this field trip. __wants__
3. <u>Several</u> (is) interested in reptiles. __are__
4. <u>Everyone</u> (hopes) the team will arrive soon. __correct__
5. <u>Much</u> (is) out of our reach. __correct__
6. <u>All</u> (is) waiting to see the school play. __are__
7. <u>Few</u> (works) as lifeguards this year. __work__
8. <u>Others</u> (walks) in the gardens. __walk__
9. <u>Everybody</u> (receives) extra credit. __correct__
10. <u>Many</u> (are writing) reports about their summer vacations. __correct__
11. <u>Either</u> of the posters (are) acceptable. __is__
12. <u>Nothing</u> about these suggestions (excite) the students more than planning a field trip! __excites__

CHAPTER 3

Principal Parts of Verbs

- Write *past*, *past participle*, or *present participle* to identify each italicized verb. Then underline the auxiliary verbs in five sentences. The first one is done for you.

1. The storm had *flown* in more quickly than we expected.   past participle
2. Rashad and I *ran* home from school to take shelter.   past
3. We saw that the storm had *blown* down a tree in front of our house.   past participle
4. Luckily, the tree *missed* our neighbor's car.   past
5. Rashad was *telling* me to make certain that all the windows were closed.   present participle
6. Together we secured the house before the storm *grew* worse.   past
7. That morning we had *seen* on the TV news that there might be a tornado warning.   past participle
8. Neither Rashad nor I *knew* what a tornado was really like.   past
9. We *decided* that the safest place in the house was the basement.   past
10. The storm was *raging* for hours, but we never saw a tornado.   present participle

- Now write a few sentences about an amusing or an unusual experience you've had related to weather. Use at least two verbs in the present participle form and circle them.

_____

Section 4.1 • 35

CHAPTER 3

Transitive and Intransitive Verbs

- Identify the underlined verb in each sentence by writing *transitive* or *intransitive* on the line.

1. In the fall (millions) of monarchs <u>fly</u> south.   intransitive
2. A female (monarch) <u>lays</u> about 400 eggs at one time.   transitive
3. A newborn monarch (caterpillar) can <u>eat</u> its own weight in food.   transitive
4. (Ladybugs) <u>use</u> their feet to smell.   transitive
5. (They) <u>chew</u> from side to side, not up and down.   intransitive
6. (Ladybugs) <u>nibble</u> aphids off rosebushes.   transitive
7. To chirp, male (crickets) <u>rub</u> their wings together.   transitive
8. Female (crickets) cannot <u>chirp</u> at all.   intransitive
9. Many (animals) <u>eat</u> crickets, including spiders, frogs, and birds.   transitive
10. Some (spiders) <u>spin</u> webs that are stronger than steel!   transitive
11. Many (spiders) <u>live</u> in dark spaces.   intransitive
12. Most spiders' (poisons) will not <u>harm</u> people.   transitive

- Now go back and read each sentence again. Circle the doer and underline the receiver (if there is one).

36 • Section 4.2

CHAPTER 3

What Makes a Good Business Letter?

- **The following business letter includes several errors. Use proofreading marks to revise it. You should find three errors in capitalization, three errors in punctuation, and one error in spelling. There are also two examples of informal or incorrect usage. Replace these words with more appropriate language.**

Jackson Junior High
33445 <u>o</u>ak Drive
Chicago, IL 12345
(123) 555-0099

Mr_⌃James Ruff
Wagging Tails Pet Sitting
<u>d</u>ogtown_⌃IL 12344
(123) 555-8833

Dear Mr. Ruff⊙

We would like to thank you for visiting our class last week to talk about your experiences in the pet-sitting business. We enjoyed hearing about your adventures in dealing with all kinds of owners and their animals, especially the potbellied pig! In fact, we would like to include a monthly column about pets in our school newspaper.

If it <s>ain't</s> **isn't** too much trouble, each month we would like to send a student to interview you. The columns could include tips for pet care, special animal stories, or information about animal health and training. In exchange for your generosity, we would be happy to help your business by placing an ad in our newspaper.

Please contact us at the phone number above if you would be interested in becoming part of our school newspaper. Thanks again for taking the time to share your knowledge and great pet stories. We look forward to hearing from <s>ya</s> **you**.

Sincerely,

Ms. Garcia

Ms. <u>g</u>arcia and the Students of Room 12
8th Grade Class
Jackson Junior High

CHAPTER 3

Troublesome Verbs

- **Circle the verb that correctly completes each sentence.**

1. I will (sit **(set)**) the box in this corner.
2. Ahmed will (learn **(teach)**) me how to use the new computer.
3. The campers have **(risen)** raised) early to start their long hike.
4. I have **(laid)** lain) clean towels on the counter for you.
5. (Bring **(Take)**) your report card home for your parents to sign.
6. He accidentally (let **(left)**) his coat at the restaurant.
7. Brett (borrowed **(lent)**) me his tools so I could fix my car.
8. Krista **(learned)** taught) about the Civil War in Mr. Smith's class.
9. Please (rise **(raise)**) the flag first every morning.
10. You may (set **(sit)**) in the chair by the window.

- **Go back and find the letter in bold type in each word you circled. Write these letters on the lines below. If your answers are correct, you will find the answer to this riddle.**

I am at the beginning of sorrow and the end of sickness. You cannot express happiness without me. I am always in risk, yet never in danger.

Answer: <u>t</u> <u>h</u> <u>e</u> <u>l</u> <u>e</u> <u>t</u> <u>t</u> <u>e</u> <u>r</u> <u>s</u>
       1 2 3 4 5 6 7 8 9 10

CHAPTER 3 Linking Verbs

- Circle eight linking verbs in the following paragraph. Then underline ten subject complements. (Hint: Subject complements are nouns, pronouns, or adjectives; they can be one word or a group of words.)

This morning the sky (appeared) clear, blue, and sunny. I imagine that the sun on my back and the wind in my hair (feel) wonderful! Today (seems) perfect for a trip to the beach. Today, however, I am in school. As I sit here daydreaming about the beach, the air (smells) fresh and the water (tastes) salty. The waves even (sound) thunderous in my ears. I could stay in this daydream forever, until I realize that the whole class is staring at me. My face (grows) hot. I guess I (was) asleep!

- What subject complements did you identify above? Find and circle these words in the word search below. Words can go across, down, or diagonally.

```
O R T A W C X L B S I E
S F R E S H R A U P E C
A T H U D J H O T D R M
L S C L E A R A L O P K
T Q U Y G E B N N P E R
Y C A D I E L S P R W
S W O N D E R F U L F D
H T U S E U A H N E G
M H I O A S N R C H
T X A S L E E P Y I T Y
```

Section 4.4 • 39

CHAPTER 3 Purpose and Tone

- Read the body paragraph from a business letter. Then write details that support the writer's purpose in the Cause-and-Effect graphic organizer. For an example of a completed Cause-and-Effect chart, see page 140.

Big Sky Airlines is the most (horrible) airline I have ever flown. I would like to get a refund of my ticket. I was (disgusted) that I had to ask three times before the flight attendant finally brought me something to drink. I was (appalled) at how rude he was to me. And then, no one seemed to have accurate information about gates and times for our arrival. We left two hours late. As I said, I would like a refund of my ticket because the entire experience was (disastrous).

What Happens	Why It Happens
Effect: Bad experience on Big Sky Airlines	Cause: I had to ask three times before getting a drink.
	Cause: The flight attendant was rude to me.
	Cause: No one had accurate information about gates and arrival times.
	Cause: We left two hours late.

- Now go back to the paragraph and circle four words that might seem too harsh for a respectful, professional business letter. On another sheet of paper, rewrite the paragraph, using your graphic organizer as a guide. Remember to use appropriate words and a courteous tone. **Answers will vary.**

40 • Lesson 2

Name _____ Date _____

CHAPTER 3
Simple, Progressive, and Perfect Tenses

- Underline the verb or verb phrase in each sentence. Write the letter that identifies the tense of the verb or verb phrase. Write *present*, *past*, or *future* to identify the action each one expresses. The first one is done for you.

  a. Simple tense   b. Progressive tense   c. Perfect tense

  1. My brother <u>studies</u> every night for two hours.   **a**   present
  2. The store <u>will be closing</u> at nine o'clock.   **b**   future
  3. We <u>are preparing</u> for next week's competition.   **b**   present
  4. The candidates <u>have posted</u> the signs for the election.   **c**   present
  5. Our class <u>will visit</u> the museum at the end of the month.   **a**   future
  6. John <u>has purchased</u> a new tire for his bicycle.   **c**   present
  7. The chores <u>will have been finished</u> by the time I get home.   **c**   future
  8. Amy <u>will have read</u> five books by the end of summer. ✓   **c**   future
  9. The researchers <u>presented</u> their findings at a public hearing.   **a**   past
  10. We <u>will be working</u> together on the science project.   **b**   future
  11. I <u>was selling</u> tickets for the student talent show.   **b**   past
  12. The issue <u>has been discussed</u> at several meetings recently. ✓   **c**   present

- Now go back and place a check next to each sentence that includes a verb in the passive voice.

42 • Section 4.6

Name _____ Date _____

CHAPTER 3
Active and Passive Voices

- If the sentence is in the active voice, rewrite it in the passive voice. If the sentence is in the passive voice, rewrite it in the active voice.
*Possible answer
  1. Leonardo da Vinci, a man of many talents, painted the *Mona Lisa*.
     The *Mona Lisa* was painted by Leonardo da Vinci, a man of many talents.*
  2. The famous *Last Supper* was also painted by Leonardo da Vinci.
     Leonardo da Vinci also painted the famous *Last Supper*.*
  3. The Louvre museum in Paris, France, displays the *Mona Lisa*.
     The *Mona Lisa* is displayed in the Louvre museum in Paris, France.*
  4. Da Vinci's notes for inventions and other ideas were written backward.
     Da Vinci wrote his notes for inventions and other ideas backward.*
  5. The Renaissance ushered in a period of rebirth in art and learning.
     A period of rebirth in art and learning was ushered in by the Renaissance.*
  6. The moons of Jupiter were discovered by the Renaissance astronomer Galileo.
     The Renaissance astronomer Galileo discovered the moons of Jupiter.*
  7. The telescope was improved by Galileo.
     Galileo improved the telescope.*
  8. Galileo believed that the sun was the center of the universe.
     That the sun was the center of the universe was believed by Galileo.*
  9. During this time it was accepted by most people that the sun revolved around the earth.
     During this time most people accepted that the sun revolved around the earth.*
  10. Galileo discovered four of Jupiter's moons.
      Four of Jupiter's moons were discovered by Galileo.*

Section 4.5 • 41

Practice Book Answers • 25

Name _____ Date _____

CHAPTER 3: Adjective and Adverb Clauses

- Rewrite each sentence by adding an adjective clause to modify the italicized nouns. Remember that an adjective clause usually begins with a relative pronoun such as *who, whom, whose, which,* or *that.* Circle the relative pronouns in your new sentences.

1. The *product* was less effective than advertised.
   Answers will vary, but students should circle the relative pronouns that they used.

2. Your *staff* provided every luxury we desired.

3. The *hotel* was more beautiful than we ever imagined.

4. I am available to speak with you at any *time*.

- Rewrite each sentence by adding an adverb clause to modify the italicized verbs. Remember that an adverb clause usually begins with a subordinate conjunction such as *than, until, because, after, before, although, as, as if,* or *unless*. Circle the subordinate conjunctions in your new sentences.

5. Before the trip started, the tour guide *spoke*.
   Answers will vary, but students should circle the subordinate conjunctions used.

6. We weren't hungry, but we *ate*.

7. The product *should be replaced*.

8. You *can watch* the game.

Name _____ Date _____

CHAPTER 3: Indicative and Imperative Moods

- Underline the verb or verb phrase in each sentence. Circle *indicative* or *imperative* to identify the mood each verb or verb phrase expresses. Then, if the sentence is indicative, rewrite it as imperative. If the sentence is imperative, rewrite it as indicative. Your new sentences can vary in meaning from the original sentences.

1. Join us for the picnic on Sunday.   indicative   **(imperative)**
   Possible answer: They are joining us for the picnic on Sunday.

2. We are planning a trip to Chile this summer.   **(indicative)**   imperative
   Possible answer: Plan a trip to Chile this summer.

3. Has Wags eaten all the food in his bowl?   **(indicative)**   imperative
   Possible answer: Eat all the food in your bowl, Wags.

4. Please bring the necessary supplies to class.   indicative   **(imperative)**
   Possible answer: He is bringing the necessary supplies to class.

5. Place the birthday gifts on this table.   indicative   **(imperative)**
   Possible answer: They are placing the birthday gifts on this table.

6. Jana is playing varsity tennis this year.   **(indicative)**   imperative
   Possible answer: Play varsity tennis this year, Jana.

- In the space below, sketch two people talking. Use speech bubbles, as in a comic book. Show one person asking a question in the indicative mood and the other answering in the imperative mood.

Sentences and sketches will vary.

CHAPTER 3: Compound Words and Clipped Words

Write the clipped form of each word below.

1. influenza — **flu**
2. automobile — **auto**
3. rhinoceros — **rhino**
4. laboratory — **lab**
5. combination — **combo**
6. necktie — **tie**
7. refrigerator — **fridge**
8. mathematics — **math**
9. statistics — **stats**
10. draperies — **drapes**
11. dormitory — **dorm**
12. preparatory — **prep**
13. graduate — **grad**
14. doctor — **doc**
15. delicatessen — **deli**

Circle the correct form of the compound word to complete each sentence. Consult a dictionary as needed.

16. Jessica is my (five year old / **five-year-old**) little sister.
17. My uncle taught me how to play (**football**) last summer.
18. How many (brother in laws / **brothers-in-law**) do you have?
19. That documentary was a real (eye opener / **eye-opener**).
20. This (**snowstorm**) snow storm) is the worst I've ever experienced.
21. Did Grandma lend you her favorite (cook book / **cookbook**)?
22. We cheered as the (fourth quarter / **fourth-quarter**) score flashed on the board.
23. Well, that's not something you see (**every day**) everyday)!
24. We will plant a row of (forget me nots / **forget-me-nots**) along the wall.

Draw a Compare and Contrast chart like the one on page 138 to compare the words *influenza* and *flu* on a separate sheet of paper.

CHAPTER 3: Subjunctive Mood

Circle the correct word choice in each sentence. Not all sentences have verbs in the subjunctive mood.

1. The director said it is necessary that the cast (**show**) shows) up on time.
2. I wish I (was / **were**) on the stage crew instead of in the chorus line.
3. The stage manager doesn't require that the crew (**be**) are) on hand all the time.
4. I know that the stage manager wouldn't be angry if I (**was**) were) late once in a while.
5. I am going to request that I (**be**) am) given time off work at the pet shelter when I'm desperately needed there.
6. My mother says that a good deed (count / **counts**) toward character building.

For each picture write a sentence that includes a verb in the subjunctive mood. Remember that the subjunctive mood refers to what is hoped or wished rather than what actually is.

7.
8.
9.
10.
11.
12.

Answers will vary.

Name _____ Date _____

CHAPTER 3: Modal Auxiliaries

- Use the modal auxiliaries in the box to write sentences on the given topics. Write the sentences as indicated in parentheses, using the underlined verbs. The first one is done for you.

| may | might | can | could |
| must | should | will | would |

*Answers will vary, but should include the following verb forms.

1. Topic: <u>Studying</u> for a midterm (necessity, present tense)
   I must study for my midterm this weekend.

2. Topic: <u>Cleaning</u> your room (obligation, past tense)
   should have cleaned*

3. Topic: <u>Watching</u> a movie (possibility, past tense)
   might have watched *or* could have watched*

4. Topic: <u>Playing</u> a soccer game (ability, present tense)
   can play*

5. Topic: <u>Borrowing</u> a sweater (permission, present tense)
   may borrow*

6. Topic: <u>Shopping</u> for a gift (intention, future tense)
   will shop*

7. Topic: <u>Finishing</u> a task (possibility, past tense)
   might have finished*

8. Topic: <u>Following</u> directions (necessity, present tense)
   must follow*

9. Topic: <u>Cooking</u> a meal (possibility, present tense)
   might cook *or* could cook*

10. Topic: <u>Finishing</u> your homework (necessity, present tense)
    must complete*

Name _____ Date _____

CHAPTER 3: Agreement of Subject and Verb—Part I

- Correct the subject-verb agreement problems in the sentences below by writing the correct form of the italicized verb on the line. If the sentence is correct as is, write *correct*.

1. *Was* you living here during the Northridge earthquake?   **Were**
2. Most people *doesn't* know what to do during an earthquake.   **don't**
3. There *are* several wildfires raging in those dry hills.   **correct**
4. A good place to hide during a tornado *are* the basement.   **is**
5. Hurricanes, as well as thunderstorms, *is* common in Florida.   **are**
6. There's *been* many <u>hurricanes</u> in Louisiana as well.   **There have been**
7. Overflowing of rivers *creates* flooding in some areas.   **correct**
8. *Are* you aware that a tsunami can follow an earthquake?   **correct**
9. Oklahoma, a Midwestern state, *experience* many tornadoes.   **experiences**
10. I *doesn't* know which state gets the most snowfall each year.   **don't**
11. *Were* you able to obtain an earthquake safety manual?   **correct**
12. *There's* several commonsense <u>rules</u> one should know.   **There are**
13. One state with historic snowfalls *are* South Dakota.   **is**
14. Alaska *don't* get sunshine during certain times of the year.   **doesn't**
15. Lightning may often *strikes* without warning.   **strike**

- Now go back and underline the subject of each italicized verb.

CHAPTER 3

Completing Forms and Writing Checks

- **Fill out the check as directed.**

On July 10, 2005, Lauren Simms bought a pair of in-line skates for $65.99. She bought them at a store called Wild Wheels. She paid with a personal check.

Lauren Simms
404 Shady Tree Lane
Hidden Oaks, TN 12233

808

Date **July 10,** 20 **05**   4-8/310

PAY TO THE ORDER OF **Wild Wheels** _____ $ **65.99**

Sixty-five and 99/100 _____ Dollars

UNIVERSAL BANK
Hidden Oaks, TN 12234

For **in-line skates**   *Lauren Simms*

000 1111 22 333 444 5 678

- **Complete this store return form for two CDs. You ordered the CDs on October 5, 2005. CD #1 was damaged in shipment. CD #2 was not the CD you ordered. You would like to receive store credit for both CDs.**

STORE RETURN FORM

MOSTLY MUSIC, Ashland, OR
Merchandise Return Form   Date: **Current date**

Billing Address: Shipping Address (if different from billing):
Full Name: **Answers will vary.**   Full Name: **Answers will vary.**
Street Address: _____   Street Address: _____
City/State/ZIP: _____   City/State/ZIP: _____

Date Merchandise Purchased: **October 5, 2005**

Title of Product #1: **Answers will vary.**   Qty: **1**   Price Each: **Answers**
Title of Product #2: **Answers will vary.**   Qty: **1**   Price Each: **will**
                                                                Total Price: **vary.**

Why are you returning the merchandise?
Product #1: **Answers will vary.**
Product #2: **Answers will vary.**

Would you like a refund, store credit, or replacement product(s)?
(circle one)   REFUND   (CREDIT)   REPLACEMENT

Signed: **Student's signature**

Voyages in English 8   Lesson 5 • 49

CHAPTER 3

Agreement of Subject and Verb—Part II

- **Circle the verb in parentheses that correctly completes each sentence.**

1. My mom and dad (is **are**) taking us on a trip to Europe.
2. Each of us (**seems** seem) interested in visiting a different country.
3. My family (**travels** travel) somewhere new each summer.
4. Another place we'd really like to visit (**is** are) China.
5. One of the museums we may (visits **visit**) is the Louvre in Paris.
6. My family and I (**leave** leaves) the first week of July.
7. Neither my brother nor I (**have** has) been out of the United States.
8. Everyone (experience **experiences**) many new and exciting adventures.
9. Germany and Spain (**are** is) the countries of our ancestry.
10. Each of us (need **needs**) to get new clothes for the trip.
11. Spanish language and culture (**was** were) my mom's major in college.
12. Our tour group (**chooses** choose) which cities to explore.
13. Two things my dad wants to see (is **are**) the Eiffel Tower and Big Ben.
14. Many of us (enjoy **enjoys**) trying different ethnic foods.

- **Now go back to the even-numbered items. Underline the first letter of each word you circled and write the letters below to answer this riddle:**

What will you break every time you name it?

Answer: **s   i   l   e   n   c   e**
         2   4   6   8 10 12 14

50 • Section 4.11   Voyages in English 8

Name _____ Date _____

CHAPTER 3 Self-Assessment

• Check *Always*, *Sometimes*, or *Never* to respond to each statement.

Writing

	Always	Sometimes	Never
I can identify a business letter and its features.			
I can identify and write all the parts of a business letter, including the date, addresses, salutation, body, closing, signature, and references.			
I can identify adjective and adverb clauses and use them to enhance my writing.			
I can identify compound words and clipped words and spell them correctly.			
I can correctly fill out checks and business forms.			
I can use the appropriate tone for a business letter, making sure to be courteous, detailed, and persuasive.			

Grammar

	Always	Sometimes	Never
I can identify the principal parts of verbs.			
I can identify and use transitive and intransitive verbs.			
I can identify troublesome verbs and use them correctly.			
I can identify and use linking verbs.			
I can identify and use verbs in the active and passive voices.			
I can identify and use verbs in the simple, progressive, and perfect tenses.			
I can identify and use verbs in the indicative, imperative, and subjunctive moods.			
I can identify and use modal auxiliaries.			
I can identify and use correct subject and verb agreement.			

• **What was the most helpful thing you learned in this chapter?**

_____

Name _____ Date _____

CHAPTER 4 Participles

• Underline the participial phrase in each sentence. Then write *present*, *past*, or *perfect* on the line to identify the tense.

1. Galloping over the hill, the chestnut stallion looks magnificent. __present__
2. The girl waiting by the door is my sister. __present__
3. Having been given a second chance, I read the speech perfectly. __perfect__
4. Hiding under the chair, the fuzzy kitten took a long nap. __present__
5. Hit with a baseball, the window shattered into hundreds of pieces. __past__
6. Kibble, having eaten the carrot, retired to the back of his cage. __perfect__
7. Having lost the game, we realized that the team needed more practice. __perfect__
8. Fiona gazed at the sun setting over the mountaintops. __present__
9. Cheering loudly, Keisha saw the team score another touchdown. __present__
10. The river flowing through the town was dangerously high. __present__
11. Loved by its new family, the stray dog had finally found a home. __past__
12. The parrot, having been taught to speak, mimicked everyone. __perfect__

• Now go back and circle the noun or pronoun each participial phrase describes.

Name _____ Date _____

CHAPTER 4
Placement of Participles

- **Identify the participle in each sentence and write it on the line. Then circle the letter in your answer that corresponds with the number. The first one is done for you.**

1. One-third of the world's ⓡequired oxygen supply is provided by rain forests.   **required**   8
2. Little light filters through the swaying trees of the canopy.   **swaying**   5
3. Chirping squirrel monkeys swing from branches overhead.   **Ⓒhirping**   1
4. Slithering snakes hunt for food.   **Slithering**   4
5. Many surviving species receive the protection of local laws.   **surⓥiving**   5
6. A rain forest's covered environment is warm and moist.   **cⓞvered**   2
7. Big cats, like the jaguar, prefer to rest in hidden places during the day.   **hiⓓden**   6
8. Most laws of protection have brought about the results wanted.   **wanteⓓ**   2
9. The endangered mandrill is almost extinct in central Africa.   **endangereⓓ**   8
10. High in the trees, a yelping toucan communicates with other birds.   **Ⓨelping**   1

- **Write the letters you circled, in order, on the lines below. If your answers are correct, you will reveal the answer to the riddle.**

In what place does yesterday always follow today?

Answer: __d__ __i__ __c__ __t__ __i__ __o__ __n__ __a__ __r__ __y__

- **Rewrite each sentence to correct the dangling or misplaced participle.**

11. Wet from the storm, I allowed our dog to come into the house.
    Possible answer: I allowed our dog, wet from the storm, to come into the house.
12. Hurrying to get to class on time, the door was already closed.
    Possible answer: Hurrying to get to class on time, I found that the door was already closed.

Section 5.2 • 53

Name _____ Date _____

CHAPTER 4
What Makes a Good Description?

- **Read the descriptive paragraph. Then answer the questions.**

> The kitchen was the heart and soul of Ana's home. It was the gathering place. This was where Ana's mama prepared love for all to share. Ana sat quietly on her stool by the counter and watched Mama move about the kitchen. Mama's slender fingers were a blur as she chopped, grated, and sliced. In her skilled, caring hands, food wasn't cooked; it was created. She didn't prepare dishes; she created masterpieces. Mama moved gracefully around the kitchen like a dancer, her long skirt swishing softly around her legs with each step. Ana watched as Mama grated fresh nutmeg into a bowl of creamy sauce. The warm air almost burst with the sweet fragrances of fresh herbs and hot spices. Boiling sauces popped softly on the stove, while onions, garlic, and peppers sizzled in a pan. Ana's mama looked up at her and smiled a knowing smile. Ana knew that one day she would dance in the kitchen, just like her mama.

*Possible answer

1. What is the mood of this passage? Why do you think so?
   The mood is warm and friendly. It is obvious that Ana admires and loves watching her mama.*

2. How does the writer help you see, smell, and hear what is happening in Mama's kitchen? Write precise words that create these images.
   I see **Mama's blurred fingers chopping, grating, and slicing; moving like a dancer; grating nutmeg into a bowl of creamy sauce; smiling at Ana***
   I smell **fresh herbs and spices; onions, garlic, and peppers cooking***
   I hear **Mama's skirt swishing softly; boiling sauces; and sizzling vegetables***

3. How did this passage make you feel?
   Answers will vary.

4. Name one comparison the writer uses to create a vivid image. Do you feel it was an effective comparison?
   food wasn't cooked, it was created; She didn't prepare dishes; she created masterpieces; Mama moved gracefully, like a dancer*

54 • Lesson 1

CHAPTER 4: Gerunds as Subjects and Complements

- Look at each picture. Then use a gerund or a gerund phrase to complete each sentence and describe the picture. *Possible answers

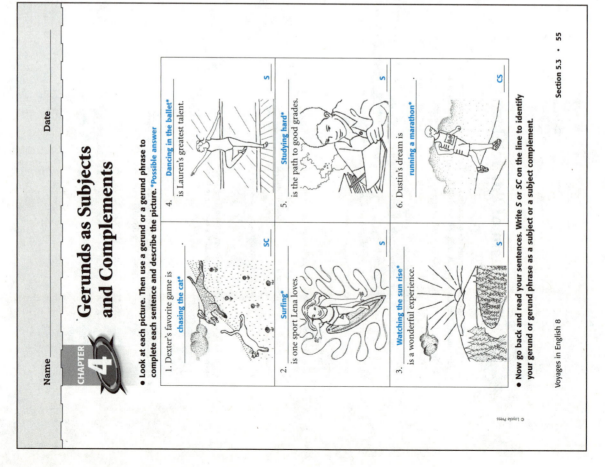

1. Dexter's favorite game is **chasing the cat**. — SC
2. **Surfing** is one sport Lena loves. — S
3. **Watching the sun rise** is a wonderful experience. — S
4. **Dancing in the ballet** is Lauren's greatest talent. — S
5. **Studying hard** is the path to good grades. — S
6. Dustin's dream is **running a marathon**. — CS

- Now go back and read your sentences. Write S or SC on the line to identify your gerund or gerund phrase as a subject or a subject complement.

CHAPTER 4: Gerunds as Objects and Appositives

- Underline the gerund phrase in each sentence. Then circle the gerund. Identify how the gerund is used by writing DO (direct object), OP (object of a preposition), or A (appositive) on the line.

1. Many people do not like giving speeches in front of large groups. — DO
2. Tanya exercises by swimming 30 laps every morning. — OP
3. Jared enjoys watching football on Sunday afternoons. — DO
4. Aerobics, exercising to music, is a popular workout at most gyms. — A
5. Amanda loves throwing parties on the weekends. — DO
6. Trey's talent, acting in the community theater, will take him far someday. — A
7. Are you the one who started using that nickname for me? — DO
8. I didn't know math skills could lead to getting so many interesting jobs. — OP
9. Jeremy began his research by reading books about motorcycles. — OP
10. Min tried drawing portraits of people rather than animals. — DO

- Find and circle the gerunds you identified above in the word search below. They can go across, down, or diagonally.

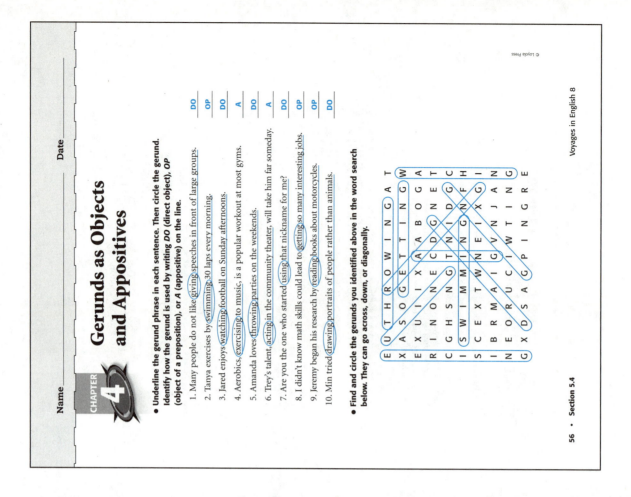

Name _____ Date _____

CHAPTER 4
Organization

- **Read each description. Write *chronological*, *spatial*, *order of importance*, or *comparison and contrast* to tell how each description is organized. Then explain your answer.**

  1. I could feel the excitement building as the game progressed. My heart was pounding so loud in my ears, I thought I would explode from the adrenaline. As I stood out in center field, I raised my face to gaze up at the clear, blue, cloudless sky. I wanted to laugh and cry at the same time. After 25 long years, our school was going to win the playoffs. I watched, spellbound, as the last pitch was thrown—strike three! The crowd exploded like a box of Fourth of July fireworks. We did it!

  Type of Organization: <u>chronological</u>

  How do you know? <u>events are told in the order they happened</u>

  2. Maui and her twin sister, Leah, are quite different. Because they are twins you would think they would be similar. Not true! Maui is a natural artist; she loves to create with her hands through painting and sketching. Leah is a natural athlete. She'd rather swing a tennis racquet or spike a volleyball than sit in front of a sketch pad. Both girls, however, enjoy reading mysteries, riding horses, and going to the beach.

  Type of Organization: <u>comparison and contrast</u>

  How do you know? <u>the paragraph described how the twins are the same and different</u>

- **Write the two types of organization that are not shown in the descriptions above.**

  3. <u>spatial</u>   4. <u>order of importance</u>

- **On a separate sheet of paper, write two descriptive paragraphs, one using each type of organization that you named on the lines above. Choose from these topics: your best friend's face, an exciting sporting event, a great party, the outside of the school.**
  <u>Answers will vary.</u>

Lesson 2 • 57

Name _____ Date _____

CHAPTER 4
Possessives with Gerunds, Using -ing Verb Forms

- **Circle the word that correctly completes each sentence.**

  1. (Amy / **Amy's**) taking an earlier flight gave her more time for sightseeing.
  2. (**Your** / You) lending me this book will save me a trip to the library.
  3. (Us / **Our**) visiting Alaska was the whole family's decision.
  4. I thought (John / **John's**) helping to create the Web site showed his commitment to the project.
  5. I hope that (**my** / me) studying hard for this exam will result in a good grade.

- **Write four different sentences using the word *winning*. Use the word as a gerund (G), a participle in a participial phrase (PP), a simple participial adjective (PA), and a progressive tense verb (PV). For example, using the word *calling*:**

  Gerund: *Calling my family* is what makes me feel good when I'm down.
  Participle in a participial phrase: The person *calling from downstairs* was my father.
  Participial adjective: Many people use *calling cards* to make long-distance phone calls.
  Progressive tense verb (past): I *was calling* my dog to come inside the house.

  *Possible answer
  Winning

	How is the word used?
<u>I couldn't believe I had the winning ticket in my hand.*</u>	PA
<u>Our poodle was winning all the top prizes at the dog show.*</u>	PV
<u>Winning the championship game was a great way to end the season.*</u>	G
<u>Winning for the first time ever, I felt a sense of accomplishment.*</u>	PP

Section 5.5

Name _____ Date _____

CHAPTER 4 — Infinitives as Subjects and Complements

• **In each sentence underline the infinitive phrase. Circle the infinitive in each phrase. Then write S (subject) or SC (subject complement) to identify how the infinitive phrase is used.**

1. An incredible act of kindness is (to adopt) a stray animal. — SC
2. Our dream is (to explore) all the countries of Africa. — SC
3. To have a working knowledge of computers is essential. — S
4. For instance, (to type) on a typewriter is basically obsolete. — S
5. To go to college is a must in my family. — S
6. My plan is (to attend) one of the Ivy League universities. — SC
7. To learn a new language is challenging but rewarding. — S
8. My idea was (to offer) more tutoring programs after school. — SC
9. Mina's greatest achievement was (to complete) her Ph.D. — SC
10. To cook all kinds of ethnic foods is my favorite hobby. — S

• **Complete each sentence with an infinitive.**

11. Something I would like to achieve is
    Answers will vary.

12. Answers will vary.
    is one of my family's traditions.

Voyages in English 8   Section 5.6 • 59

Name _____ Date _____

CHAPTER 4 — Graphic Organizers

• Use the Venn diagram to compare and contrast elementary school and junior high school. Write ideas that apply only to elementary school in the larger section of the left circle. Write ideas that apply only to junior high in the larger section of the right circle. Write the ways both schools are the same in the overlapping middle section.

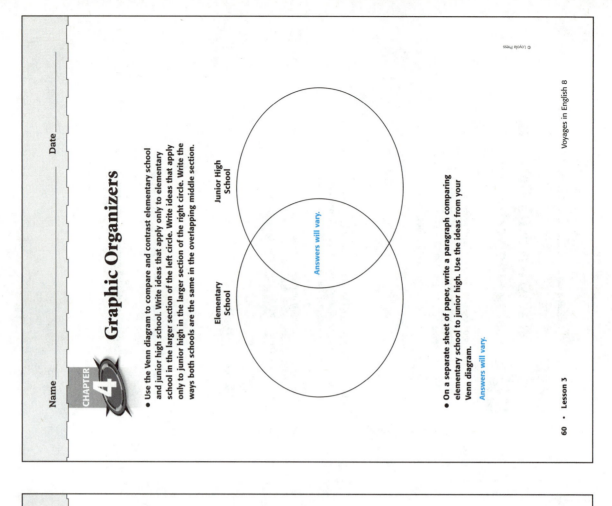

Elementary School   Junior High School

Answers will vary.

• On a separate sheet of paper, write a paragraph comparing elementary school to junior high. Use the ideas from your Venn diagram.
  Answers will vary.

60 • Lesson 3   Voyages in English 8

Name _____ Date _____

CHAPTER 4 — Infinitives as Objects

• Underline the infinitive in each sentence. Then circle the verb of which it is the direct object.

1. Mr. Hale (encouraged) us to brainstorm ideas for the club's fundraiser.
2. Shyla's horse (started) to gallop at full speed over the rocky pathway.
3. Our kittens (decided) to escape the rain by hiding under the house.
4. We (mean) to find old letters and journals in my grandparents' attic.
5. Tom (expects) to be the first runner across the finish line.
6. Mia (wanted) to alleviate the sick child's discomfort.
7. How did you (manage) to finish all that paperwork?
8. My sister (needed) me to help her with a special birthday dinner.
9. After practice, he (likes) to exercise for several hours in the gym.

• Write each infinitive below in a complete sentence. Use each infinitive as a direct object.

10. to climb **Answers will vary.**
11. to sing **Answers will vary.**
12. to be **Answers will vary.**

Section 5.7 • 61

Name _____ Date _____

CHAPTER 4 — Infinitives as Appositives

• From the list below, choose the appositive that best completes each sentence. Then circle the noun it explains.

Infinitive Choices
R. to become a professional ice skater
E. to win the district championship
I. to procrastinate constantly
D. to interview our grandparents
N. to make balloon animals
H. to sell everything at 50 percent off
A. to give an oral report
C. to construct a new hospital
G. to take roll at the beginning of class

1. It was her ultimate (dream) __R__.
2. Our team's (hope), __E__, was finally achieved.
3. The builders' (plan), __C__, was stopped by local landowners.
4. Mr. Greer's (assignment), __D__, helped us learn about history.
5. My (tendency), __I__, means that I must rush to meet deadlines.
6. Our carnival booth's (activity), __N__, delighted all the children.
7. It is Daniel's (turn), __G__.
8. Our final (reduction), __H__, helped to empty the store.
9. Her biggest (fear), __A__, was overcome by taking a speech class.

• Now write the letters on the lines below. If your answers are correct, you will reveal the answer to the riddle.

What do you have when 20 rabbits step backward?

Answer: A R E C E D I N G   H A R E   L I N E!
        1 2 3 4 5 6 7   8 9

62 • Section 5.8

CHAPTER 4

Thesaurus

- **Use a thesaurus to find a more precise or vivid word to replace each underlined word.**

Did you know that animals traveled into space before people did? It's true! Animals led the way in space exploration. Scientists wanted to make certain that animals could (1) <u>live</u> in space before humans attempted the trip. The first animals to survive a (2) <u>trip</u> into space were a monkey and eleven mice. They rode in a rocket straight up into space and down again. The mission was a success. The most (3) <u>well-known</u> animal of all, however, is Ham the chimpanzee. He actually (4) <u>worked</u> for his mission by learning how to pull certain levers during the space flight. Each time he correctly pulled a lever, he would (5) <u>get</u> a banana pellet!

1. Possible answer: **survive**
2. Possible answer: **journey**
3. Possible answer: **famous**
4. Possible answer: **trained**
5. Possible answer: **receive**

- **Circle the word in parentheses that best replaces the underlined word in each sentence. Look up any words you don't understand in a dictionary to make sure you choose the most accurate word.**

6. Tera felt <u>weak</u> after not eating all day. (fragile (frail) soft)
7. Jamal <u>gave</u> many hours to volunteer work. (supplied granted (contributed))
8. Siena <u>tried</u> to finish the painting before the end of class. (struggled (attempted) strained)
9. The <u>crafty</u> fox slid into the henhouse before anyone could see it. ((cunning) smooth artful)
10. He awoke, startled and <u>scared</u>, at the sound of the loud crash. (intimidated anxious (frightened))

CHAPTER 4

Infinitives as Adjectives

- **Underline the infinitive phrase used as an adjective in each sentence. Then write the noun or pronoun it describes.**

1. The street <u>to take to the mall</u> goes near our school.   **street**
2. She is always the one <u>to bring delicious, homemade desserts</u>.   **one**
3. The first reference <u>to consult for maps</u> is an atlas.   **reference**
4. I bought a ticket <u>to ride the roller coaster at the ticket booth</u>.   **ticket**
5. This health manual outlines a myriad of ways <u>to exercise</u>.   **ways**
6. The horse <u>to ride in the parade</u> is that beautiful chestnut.   **horse**
7. The kitten <u>to adopt</u> is the striped one in that big basket.   **kitten**
8. The person <u>to watch in the game</u> is the quarterback.   **person**
9. Myra knew she didn't have time <u>to finish the essay</u>.   **time**
10. Acceptable guests <u>to invite to the classroom</u> are listed on the board.   **guests**

- **Search a newspaper. Find three infinitive phrases that are used as adjectives. Cut out the articles and underline the phrases. Share them with a partner.**

Name _____ Date _____

CHAPTER 4 — Infinitives as Adverbs

- Read the paragraph. Go back and underline six infinitive phrases used as adverbs. Then draw an arrow from each phrase to the verb, adjective, or adverb it describes. Identify the word by writing *V* (verb), *ADJ* (adjective), or *ADV* (adverb) above it.

Last summer I went to Washington, D.C., **to visit our nation's capital**. I was
                                                    V
thrilled **to see** many original documents written by presidents of the past. After
ADJ
viewing the Washington monument, I visited the Capitol **to learn more about
our country's government**. It was beautiful! I felt extremely patriotic as I walked
                                                  ADJ
the grand hallways. I also visited the White House, and I was excited **to see the
place where our president and his family live**. I listened to the tour guide talk
about all the famous people who had stayed there at one time or another. Next,
                       V
I traveled to the Lincoln Memorial **to admire the statue of my favorite president,
Abraham Lincoln**. I was not in Washington long enough **to see everything on my
                                              ADV
sightseeing list**, but I still had a great time!

- Now write two sentences about one museum, building, monument, or place that you have seen or that you would like to see in Washington, D.C. Include an infinitive used as an adverb in each sentence.

Answers will vary.

Name _____ Date _____

CHAPTER 4 — Figurative Language

- Write *simile* or *metaphor* to identify the comparison in each sentence. Then underline the two things being compared. The first one is done for you.

1. My big black <u>cat</u> slithers around my ankles like a <u>snake</u>.   simile
2. <u>She</u> was a graceful <u>swan</u> when she danced.   **metaphor**
3. The <u>baseball</u> shot out of the park like a <u>rocket</u>.   **simile**
4. Our <u>school</u> was a <u>zoo</u> during graduation ceremonies.   **metaphor**
5. My <u>skin</u> was as rough as <u>sandpaper</u> after working in the sun.   **simile**
6. My <u>teacher</u> is a <u>hawk</u> circling the classroom during exams.   **metaphor**
7. Snarling like a <u>lion</u>, the <u>quarterback</u> leapt into the end zone.   **simile**
8. Javier's old <u>dog</u> is still as playful and silly as a young <u>pup</u>.   **simile**
9. Her gentle <u>words</u> were pearls of <u>wisdom</u> to us all.   **metaphor**
10. Like a <u>bloodhound</u>, <u>he</u> guided us through the thick forest.   **simile**

- Use hyperbole or personification to write a sentence about each topic.

11. trees   **Answers will vary.**

12. baby   **Answers will vary.**

CHAPTER 4: Hidden and Split Infinitives

• Find the hidden infinitive in each sentence. Underline the infinitive and circle the word that helped you find it.

1. Santiago (heard) the wind whip violently through the treetops.
2. We (need) not use your truck for our camping trip this weekend.
3. We could (see) the dancers float across the stage like angels.
4. Can you (help) me move into my new apartment this weekend?
5. Our dog does not (dare) enter the house when his paws are muddy.
6. Dad (made) the neighborhood children clean the yard after their games.
7. Stella does nothing (but) talk on the phone to her boyfriend.
8. She would prefer to read (than) participate in sports.

• Rewrite each sentence to eliminate the split infinitive.

9. Ms. Cardoza asked me to completely redesign my science project.
   Possible answer: Ms. Cardoza asked me to redesign my science project completely.
10. My brother asked us to not enter his room without knocking.
    Possible answer: My brother asked us not to enter his room without knocking.
11. Loc stubbornly decided to not cooperate with the rest of the team.
    Possible answer: Loc stubbornly decided not to cooperate with the rest of the team.
12. We asked Mom to quickly show us our list of weekend chores.
    Possible answer: We asked Mom to show us our list of weekend chores quickly.

Section 5.11 • 67

CHAPTER 4: Self-Assessment

• Check *Always*, *Sometimes*, or *Never* to respond to each statement.

Writing	Always	Sometimes	Never
I can identify descriptive writing and its features.			
I understand how to effectively organize the details in a descriptive paragraph.			
I can use graphic organizers, such as Venn diagrams and word webs, to organize my ideas.			
I can use a thesaurus to find more vivid and precise words.			
I can identify and use figurative language.			
I include all the key features when I write a description.			

Grammar	Always	Sometimes	Never
I can identify and use participles.			
I can identify and correct dangling and misplaced participles.			
I can identify and use gerunds used as subjects and complements.			
I can identify and use gerunds used as objects and appositives.			
I can identify and use possessives with gerunds.			
I can distinguish gerunds from participles and verbs.			
I can identify and use infinitives as subjects and complements.			
I can identify and use infinitives as objects.			
I can identify and use infinitives as appositives.			
I can identify and use infinitives as adjectives.			
I can identify and use infinitives as adverbs.			
I can identify and use hidden infinitives.			
I can identify and eliminate split infinitives.			

• Write the most helpful thing you learned in this chapter.

_____

68 • Chapter 4 Self-Assessment

CHAPTER 5: Types of Adverbs

- **Circle the adverb in each sentence. Then choose its type from the box and write it on the line.**

Types of Adverbs

| time | place | manner |
| degree | affirmation | negation |

1. The train moved (forward) with a screeching jolt. — **place**
2. We (frequently) spend time at the beach. — **time**
3. Cara searched (frantically) for her lost backpack. — **manner**
4. The spotlight from the helicopter is (quite) bright. — **degree**
5. The elephants trumpeted (loudly) as they stampeded. — **manner**
6. Bailey would (never) catch the football. — **negation**
7. Molly sat (there) while I practiced my speech. — **place**
8. The principal's speech was (extremely) long but entertaining. — **degree**
9. She (seldom) gets a poor grade on a test. — **time**
10. I (certainly) did expect the whole team to attend. — **affirmation**
11. Handle those valuable ceramics (carefully). — **manner**
12. Antonio (often) gives to charities that help animals. — **time**

- **Write two sentences about members of your family using adverbs of manner. Circle the adverb in each sentence.**

13. **Answers will vary.**
14.

Voyages in English 8 • Section 6.1 • 69

CHAPTER 5: Interrogative Adverbs and Adverbial Nouns

- **Underline the adverbial nouns in the sentences.**

1. At the store, we bought eggs and one quart of milk.
2. My teacher allowed 20 minutes to finish the test.
3. We drove more than 1,800 miles across country last summer.
4. We traveled south for the holidays, from Minnesota to Texas.
5. Our plane flew east, carrying us from Oregon to New York.
6. Tyra added two cups of flour to the cookie batter.
7. Our big, fluffy cat weighs 13 pounds.
8. We estimated three feet to each meter.
9. My dad gave us each 75 cents to buy ice cream.
10. The paper clip was so light it didn't even weigh an ounce.

- **Write a conjunction or an interrogative adverb to complete each sentence. Write C for conjunction or I for interrogative on the line.**

11. Tomorrow is the day **when** we hold the annual school Olympics. — **C**
12. **When** did you place the freshly baked cookies? — **I**
13. Summer is the time **when** many families take trips. — **C**
14. This is the building **where** we chose to hold the awards. — **C**
15. **Why** are those students always late to class? — **I**

70 • Section 6.2 • Voyages in English 8

CHAPTER 5

Comparative and Superlative Adverbs

- Revise each sentence by writing the correct positive, comparative, or superlative form of the italicized adverb.

1. The tomcat ran *more faster* than the dog. __faster__
2. Tia threw the ball *most farthest* than anyone else on the team. __farther__
3. My best friend sings *most beautifully* than I do. __more beautifully__
4. Josh finished the test *quickly* than Corina. __more quickly__
5. Evan works *most hardest* of anyone. __hardest__
6. The tiny mouse quivered *less nervous* than it did the day before. __less nervously__
7. My teacher gives instructions *most carefully* for each assignment. __carefully__
8. Those two rabbits frolic *playfully* than the others. __more playfully__
9. Of everyone in our speech class, she speaks *more intelligently*. __most intelligently__
10. The tired baby cried *loudly* than her twin sister. __louder__
11. I arrived at the party *most latest* than my friends. __later__
12. Of all the players on the team, Liz catches *better*. __best__

- Write two sentences about your day so far. Use a comparative adverb in the first sentence and a superlative adverb in the second one.

13. __Answers will vary.__
14.

CHAPTER 5

What Makes a Good Expository Essay?

- Good expository writing has a main idea clearly stated in a topic sentence. This sentence is then supported by facts, data, statistics, and examples. Read the following paragraph, and then complete the paragraph plan. For an example of a paragraph plan, see page 139.

The Declaration of Independence, written and signed in 1776, was a revolutionary document for its time. This document declared that the colonies in America were free from British rule. The colonists considered themselves free and independent. The document also stated that the colonists wanted to govern themselves as a new nation. They were declaring their freedom as well as expressing the revolutionary idea that all people have certain rights that cannot be taken away by a government or ruler. The ideas in the Declaration of Independence were seen as so revolutionary that the British claimed the document was treasonous. The Revolutionary War began shortly thereafter.

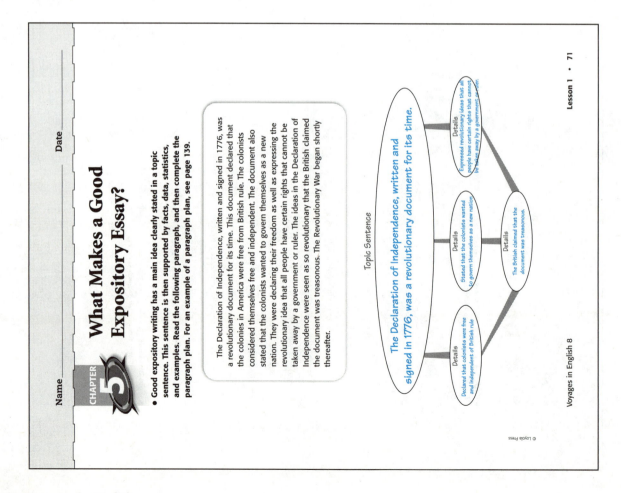

Topic Sentence: The Declaration of Independence, written and signed in 1776, was a revolutionary document for its time.

Details: Declared that colonists were free and independent of British rule

Details: Stated that the colonists wanted to govern themselves as a new nation

Details: The British claimed that the document was treasonous.

Details: Expressed revolutionary ideas that all people have certain rights that cannot be taken away by a government or ruler.

Name _____ Date _____

CHAPTER 5: Fact and Opinion

● Read each statement. Write *fact* if the statement is a fact or *opinion* if it is an opinion.

1. Dogs are significantly easier to train than cats. __opinion__
2. Mercury's orbit around the sun is shorter than that of Earth. __fact__
3. People who eat healthful foods live longer lives. __opinion__
4. Thomas Jefferson signed the Declaration of Independence. __fact__
5. Our football team won the state championship last year. __fact__
6. High school athletes do better in school than nonathletes. __opinion__
7. Because of the crowds, summer is the worst time to visit Europe. __opinion__
8. My parents will send me to the college of my choice. __opinion__
9. My mother is a truly talented lawyer. __opinion__
10. You have to receive a law degree in order to practice law. __fact__
11. Leonardo da Vinci painted *The Last Supper* and the *Mona Lisa*. __fact__
12. The Renaissance was a time of wonderful art and new ideas. __opinion__

● Write one fact and one opinion about each topic.

13. My best friend
    Fact: __Answers will vary.__
    Opinion: _____
14. My favorite song
    Fact: _____
    Opinion: _____

74 • Lesson 2   Voyages in English 8

Name _____ Date _____

CHAPTER 5: As . . . As, So . . . As, and Equally

● Write *as*, *so*, or *equally* to complete each sentence.

1. This dress is not __so or as__ expensive as the ones on that rack.
2. The two students are __equally__ matched for the competition.
3. The peak of Mt. Whitney isn't nearly __so or as__ high as that of Mt. Everest.
4. I can juggle __as__ many balls as the juggler at the fair.
5. She can't read __so or as__ quickly as the rest of the group.
6. The dancers are __equally__ trained for classical ballet.
7. The amateur musicians played __as__ skillfully as the professionals.
8. Today's hike is __as__ difficult as yesterday's hike.

● Write a sentence that includes *as . . . as* or *so . . . as* for each topic.

9. Your friend tells a funnier joke than you do
   Possible answer: **My joke wasn't so (or as) funny as my friend's joke.**
10. The championship game was more exciting last year
    Possible answer: **This year's championship game is not so (or as) exciting as last year's.**
11. Both the pizza and the spaghetti are spicy
    Possible answer: **The pizza is as spicy as the spaghetti.**
12. Your class collected the same amount of cans for the food drive as you did last year
    Possible answer: **My class collected as many cans for the food drive as it did last year.**

Voyages in English 8   Section 6.4 • 73

Practice Book Answers • 41

Name _____ Date _____

CHAPTER 5
Adverb Phrases and Clauses

- **Underline the adverb phrases and clauses in the paragraph. Then circle the word each phrase or clause describes.**

Last summer, my family (traveled) to Italy. Because we had just one week to spend, we (planned) to visit only three cities. Our first stop was Venice. We took a gondola ride and (cruised) through the canals. Then we visited St. Mark's Square and (gazed) in wonder. We (walked) until our feet were sore. Our next stop was Florence. I could (see), as we traveled through the city, many beautiful representations of Florentine art. When I saw Michelangelo's statue of David, I (realized) what a masterpiece it really was. We could hardly wait to explore Rome, our final stop. Our flight (arrived) late in the evening. We immediately (went) to the Trevi Fountain. I (threw) in a coin so that I could ensure my return someday.

- **Write a short paragraph about a special place you have visited. Include at least four adverb phrases or clauses. Then underline the phrases or clauses and circle the words they describe.**

Answers will vary.

_____
_____
_____
_____
_____
_____
_____

Name _____ Date _____

CHAPTER 5
Single and Multiword Prepositions

- **Circle the two prepositions in each sentence.**

1. The juice (from) the grapes (on) the vine was sweet.
2. We put all the pickles (into) the barrel (behind) the barn.
3. I saw hundreds (of) stars (through) my new telescope.
4. I placed a flower (in) the vase and tucked one (behind) my ear.
5. The park (near) my house features free concerts (during) the summer.

- **Circle the multiword prepositions in the following sentences.**

6. (In spite of) the heat we spent the day at the beach.
7. (On account of) the cloudy skies I couldn't see Saturn.
8. Please back the car (out of) the garage for me.
9. I decided to concentrate on rain forest insects (instead of) snakes in my report.
10. (Because of) the heavy snowfall school closed for the day.

- **Choose the correct preposition to complete each sentence. Write it on the line.**

| according to | toward | after | in spite of | between |

11. The kittens slept __between__ the mother cat and the fireplace.
12. We went out to dinner __after__ seeing the movie.
13. The plane began its slow ascent __toward__ the cloud-filled sky.
14. The baseball game continued __in spite of__ the rain.
15. __According to__ newspaper reports, the hurricane hit at 2:30 a.m.

Name _____ Date _____

CHAPTER 5
Evaluating Web Sites

• Choose the best keyword (or words) to enter into your search engine to research each topic.

1. The number of cheetahs living in Africa
   a. African wildlife (c.) cheetah population
   b. wildcats d. cheetahs

2. The meaning and history of your family's name
   (a.) name etymology c. family history
   b. family names d. names

3. The last five winners of the Best Picture Oscar at the Academy Awards
   a. best picture (c.) Academy Awards statistics
   b. academy awards d. movie trivia

4. Important battles that turned the tide in the Civil War
   a. Civil War facts (d.) Civil War battles
   b. great battles c. Civil War

5. Most recent theories on why dinosaurs became extinct
   a. dinosaur history c. prehistoric creatures
   (b.) dinosaur extinction d. dinosaurs

• Write the letter of the domain extension you would look for in a URL (web address) to find information on each topic.

a.	gov
b.	edu
c.	mil
d.	org
e.	com

6. History of the American flag — **a**
7. List of ranks in the Navy — **c**
8. Jets used by the U.S. Navy — **c**
9. College class offerings — **b**
10. Registering to vote — **a**
11. Ford trucks — **e**
12. Postage rates — **a**
13. University campus map — **b**
14. ASPCA animal adoptions — **d**
15. Disneyland's hours of operation — **e**

Lesson 3 • 77

Name _____ Date _____

CHAPTER 5
Troublesome Prepositions

• Circle the preposition that correctly completes each sentence.

1. How did you decide ((between) among) red and pink shoes?
2. Taylor was angry ((with) at) Elijah for forgetting her birthday.
3. We differ (with (on)) the types of clothes we like.
4. Her new kitten looks ((like) as if) a tiger.
5. We will choose (between (among)) five students for class president.
6. This car differs (with (from)) that one in size and speed.
7. Sean is angry ((at) with) the idea of being late again.
8. He looked (like (as if)) he was going to scream.
9. Carlos differs ((with) on) Mom over the college he will attend.
10. Please put the lamp (besides (beside)) the chair.

• Use the prepositions *differ with*, *differ on*, and *differ from* in three sentences. Write about a disagreement with a friend or family member.

11. Answers will vary.
12. _____
13. _____

78 • Section 7.2

Practice Book Answers • 43

Name _____ Date _____

CHAPTER 5: Words Used as Adverbs and Prepositions

- Write *preposition* or *adverb* to identify how each italicized word is used.

1. Above us, the jets streaked *across* the sky. _____preposition_____
2. The loud noise caused us to look *up*. _____adverb_____
3. How many jets swept *over* the throngs of people? _____preposition_____
4. The crowd cheered when one jet rolled *over*. _____adverb_____
5. We moved *toward* the airplanes to get a better view. _____preposition_____
6. Now, I could see everything *around* me. _____preposition_____
7. I heard a loud boom as another jet flew *past*. _____adverb_____
8. The jet must have flown directly *over*. _____adverb_____
9. A loud cheer erupted *from* the people in the crowd. _____preposition_____
10. After the show, we all went *inside*. _____adverb_____

- Circle the object of each word in italic type you identified as a preposition. Write the first letter of each word in order on the lines. If your answers are correct, you will reveal the answer to the riddle.

What sits in a corner while traveling all around the world?

Answer: A <u>s</u> <u>t</u> <u>a</u> <u>m</u> <u>p</u>
         1 2 3 4 5

Name _____ Date _____

CHAPTER 5: Noun Clauses

- Rewrite each sentence so that it contains a noun clause. Use the word in parentheses to begin the noun clause. Remember, a noun clause can be a subject, an object, a complement, or an appositive. The first one is done for you. *Possible answer.

1. They couldn't decide on the fair or the museum. (whether)
   They couldn't decide whether they should go to fair or to the museum.

2. I want us to visit New York City this summer, and it is my dream. (that)
   It is my dream that we visit New York City this summer.   OR   That we visit New York City this summer is my dream.

3. The manual explains the construction of the telescope. (how)
   The manual explains how you can construct the telescope.

4. I read 10 books over the summer, and that is a fact. (that)
   It is a fact that I read 10 books over the summer.   OR   That I read 10 books over the summer is a fact.

5. I could see the deer, and I was standing in the meadow. (where)
   I could see the deer from where I was standing in the meadow.   OR   From where I was standing in the meadow I could see the deer.

6. We didn't know what to make for dinner, so it was up for debate. (what)
   What we should make for dinner was up for debate.

- Use the following noun clauses in sentences of your own.

7. that he was the most talented athlete
   Answers will vary. _____

8. how to get to the campground _____

9. what we needed to know _____

10. that the party had started without us _____

CHAPTER 5 — Prepositional Phrases as Adjectives

- Underline the adjective phrase in each sentence. Then identify the word it describes by writing it on the line.

1. Our oceans contain almost countless types of sharks. — **types**
2. A shark has many tiny holes on its head that help it find prey. — **holes**
3. These holes, *ampullae of Lorenzini*, help sharks detect electric signals. — **ampullae**
4. The eyes of most sharks are extremely sensitive. — **eyes**
5. The Great White Shark is one of the most well-known species. — **one**
6. The lifespan for this shark can reach 100 years. — **lifespan**
7. Some books about sharks have frightened people. — **books**
8. In fact, most sharks don't want interaction with people. — **interaction**
9. Sharks first appeared eons before the time that today's fish appeared. — **eons**
10. The time before the dinosaur's period is when sharks first developed. — **time**
11. The teeth in a shark's mouth are razor-sharp and tilted inward. — **teeth**
12. Extinction of the giant Megalodon shark occurred approximately 1.6 million years ago. — **Extinction**
13. Great White Sharks grow new rows of teeth every one or two weeks. — **rows**
14. The males of the species are usually smaller than the females. — **males**

- Write the first letter of the boxed words in order on the lines. If your answers are correct, you will reveal the answer to the riddle.

What occurs once in a minute, twice in a moment, but never in an hour?

Answer: t h e   l e t t e r   m

Section 7.4 • 81

CHAPTER 5 — Prepositional Phrases as Adverbs

- Underline the adverb phrase in each sentence. Then write the word (or words) the adverb phrase describes.

1. During the Middle Ages many boys wanted to be knights. — **wanted**
2. You may wonder about a boy's path to knighthood. — **wonder**
3. Usually, a boy started as a page, a knight's assistant. — **started**
4. A page learned courtly manners early in his training. — **early**
5. He was loyal to his knight. — **loyal**
6. At the age of 14, a page became a squire. — **became**
7. Squires assisted knights with their horses, spurs, and weapons. — **assisted**
8. During this training, a squire worked extremely hard every day. — **worked**
9. After seven years a successful squire was usually knighted. — **was knighted**
10. To confer knighthood, a nobleman dubbed the squire on the shoulders, using a sword. — **dubbed**
11. The new knight would always act with bravery and honesty. — **would act**
12. A knight served his king with loyalty for life. — **served**

- Sketch a picture showing one scene described above. Write a sentence about your picture, using an adverb phrase.

82 • Section 7.5

Practice Book Answers • 45

CHAPTER 5 Prefixes

- **Identify the meaning of the underlined prefix in each group of words. Write the meaning on the line. Refer to the box as needed. You will not use all of the meanings.**

Prefix Meanings			
two	not	opposite	to/toward	against	surpassing
too much	back/again	less than	together	bad	many/much
life	before	three	between	one	with

1. i<u>l</u>legal, i<u>l</u>literate, i<u>l</u>logical _____not_____
2. <u>inter</u>woven, <u>inter</u>connect, <u>inter</u>change _____between_____
3. <u>bi</u>annual, <u>bi</u>form, <u>bi</u>coastal _____two_____
4. <u>anti</u>bacterial, <u>anti</u>toxic, <u>anti</u>terrorist _____against_____
5. <u>multi</u>faceted, <u>multi</u>use, <u>multi</u>media _____many/much_____
6. <u>mis</u>take, <u>mis</u>manage, <u>mis</u>inform _____bad_____
7. <u>pre</u>plan, <u>pre</u>nuptual, <u>pre</u>order _____before_____
8. <u>out</u>pace, <u>out</u>wait, <u>out</u>rank _____surpassing_____
9. <u>over</u>heated, <u>over</u>wrought, <u>over</u>emotional _____too much_____
10. <u>re</u>match, <u>re</u>iterate, <u>re</u>evaluate _____back/again_____
11. <u>mono</u>layer, <u>mono</u>rail, <u>mono</u>culture _____one_____
12. <u>dis</u>trust, <u>dis</u>allow, <u>dis</u>order _____opposite_____

- **Now use the prefixes and meanings above to write a word that matches each definition.**

13. To read again _____reread_____
14. To determine before _____predetermine_____
15. Badly spelled _____misspelled_____

Voyages in English 8   Lesson 5 • 83

CHAPTER 5 Prepositional Phrases as Nouns

- **Underline the noun phrase in each sentence. Write S if the phrase acts as a subject. Write SC if the phrase acts as a subject complement.**

1. <u>Under the tree</u> is my favorite place to read a book. _____S_____
2. Because of the snow was the reason we had to cancel the play. _____SC_____
3. The spot where we should make our campsite is <u>over this mountain</u>. _____SC_____
4. Beside that meadow was where we saw deer. _____SC_____
5. <u>In front of that trail</u> is the location where we saw the black bear. _____S_____
6. A bad time to talk on the phone is during a lightning storm. _____SC_____
7. <u>Toward the beach</u> is the direction we should head next. _____S_____
8. My favorite place to nap was among those wildflowers. _____SC_____

- **Fill in each of the blanks with a prepositional noun phrase.**

1. _____ is where she put the dirty dishes.
2. _____ is my favorite time of day.
3. The reason we rode our bikes is _____.
4. _____ is the best place to watch a baseball game.
5. My normal time for watching TV is _____.
6. _____ is my favorite place to relax.
7. My favorite time to eat pizza is _____.
8. _____ is where we spotted the squirrel.

Answers will vary, but answers should be prepositional noun phrases.

84 • Section 7.6   Voyages in English 8

CHAPTER 6 Kinds of Sentences

- Identify each sentence by writing *declarative, interrogative, imperative,* or *exclamatory.*

1. My best friend gave me a watch for my birthday. — declarative
2. Did Andrea remember to walk the dog? — interrogative
3. Please help with the chores this weekend. — imperative
4. That was an incredible game! — exclamatory
5. The grainy sand felt warm between my toes. — declarative
6. Is Noah a good tennis player? — interrogative
7. What an amazing adventure you had! — exclamatory
8. Come with me to play tennis this afternoon. — imperative

- Draw a line between each complete subject and complete predicate. Underline the simple subject once and circle the simple predicate.

9. All kinds of animals | <u>are trained</u> to perform tricks.
10. Brandon's talented <u>dog</u> | (does) a lot of funny tricks.
11. <u>Prentiss</u> | (can catch) balls in the air.
12. Trained <u>horses</u> | (jump) fences as part of a competition.
13. My friend's Persian <u>cat</u> | (fetches) pom-poms on command.
14. Many <u>people</u> | (watch) killer whales and dolphins in shows at amusement parks.
15. The amazing <u>dolphin</u> | (might be) one of the smartest animals on earth.

Section 8.1

CHAPTER 5 Self-Assessment

- Check *Always, Sometimes,* or *Never* to respond to each statement.

Writing

	Always	Sometimes	Never
I can identify expository writing and its features.			
I can identify facts and opinions.			
I can effectively locate topics on the Internet and evaluate web sites.			
I can identify and use noun clauses.			
I can use prefixes to understand word meanings.			
I include all the key features when I write an expository piece.			

Grammar

	Always	Sometimes	Never
I can identify and use different types of adverbs.			
I can identify and use adverbial nouns.			
I can form and use comparative and superlative adverbs.			
I can use *as . . . as, so . . . as,* and *equally.*			
I can identify and use adverb phrases and clauses.			
I can identify and use single and multiword prepositions.			
I can use troublesome prepositions correctly.			
I can identify and use adverbs and prepositions.			
I can identify and use prepositional phrases as adjectives.			
I can identify and use prepositional phrases as adverbs.			
I can identify and use prepositional phrases as nouns.			

- Write the most helpful thing you learned in this chapter.

Chapter 5 Self-Assessment

Practice Book Answers • 47

Name _____ Date _____

CHAPTER 6
Adjective and Adverb Phrases

- **Underline the adjective or adverb phrase in each sentence. On the first line, write PREP for prepositional, PART for participial, or INF for infinitive. On the second line, write ADV for adverb or ADJ for adjective.**

1. These signs are part <u>of a special pet adoption program</u>. **PREP** **ADJ**

2. The shelter's special pet adoption program began <u>in 2000</u>. **PREP** **ADV**

3. Many people donate their time <u>to help the shelter staff</u>. **INF** **ADV**

4. <u>Gaining local popularity</u>, the shelter receives many donations. **PART** **ADJ**

5. Many animals in the shelter need immediate medical care. <u>(blank)</u> **PREP** **ADJ**

6. There is never money enough <u>to pay for needed services</u>. **INF** **ADV**

7. Veterinarians volunteer <u>to treat sick and hurt animals</u>. **INF** **ADV**

8. <u>Expanding its services</u>, the shelter recently began taking reptiles. **PART** **ADJ**

9. The shelter is a good place <u>to bring kittens and puppies</u>. **INF** **ADJ**

10. Every animal eventually is placed <u>in a good home</u>. **PREP** **ADV**

11. The best program is the one <u>with free spaying and neutering</u>. **PREP** **ADJ**

12. Every animal there is treated <u>with love and care</u>. **PREP** **ADV**

Section 8.2 • 87

Name _____ Date _____

CHAPTER 6
What Makes Good Persuasive Writing?

- **Read this essay. Then answer the questions.**

> The Bengal tiger is disappearing at an alarming rate. Like other species that have been brought back from near extinction, this animal must be saved. It is estimated that there are fewer than 3,000 Bengal tigers left in the wild! There are several reasons for this. The primary reason is that tigers are heavily hunted for sport, even though it is outlawed.
>
> Also, an increase in human population and farming has caused the tiger to lose large areas of natural habitat. In India, a government program called Project Tiger was established more than 30 years ago. It now has 23 sanctuaries established for tigers. Even though this wonderful program has made great contributions to saving the tiger, it cannot solve the overall problem.
>
> The human population continues to grow, and the tigers continue to disappear. It is imperative that we protect these beautiful animals.

1. What is the author's position statement?

   The Bengal tiger must be saved

2. List two facts that support the author's position.
   Possible answers: It is estimated that there are fewer than 3,000 Bengal tigers left in the wild. Tigers are heavily hunted for sport, even though it is outlawed. An increase in human population and farming has caused the tiger to lose large areas of natural habitat as well as prey animals. The human population continues to grow, and tigers are again disappearing

3. List two opinions that support the author's position.
   Possible answers: Some animals on our planet are disappearing at an alarming rate. The primary reason is that tigers are heavily hunted for sport. Even though this wonderful program has made great contributions to saving the tiger, it cannot solve the overall problem. It is imperative that we find better ways to protect these beautiful animals

- **Choose a position statement from below. Then set up your ideas in a problem/solution chart that you write on a separate sheet of paper. For an example problem/solution chart, see page 140. Answers will vary.**

  - Our school should have a shorter school day.
  - Students should choose their own lunch menus.
  - All students should join a sports team or club.
  - I should be student body president.

88 • Lesson 1

CHAPTER 6 Adjective Clauses

- **Write the adjective clause from the box that best completes each sentence. Underline the noun or pronoun each clause describes.**

where he works as a chef	where people surf	that I read about
whose team won the game	which is my best subject	that I drove
where people camp	who taught me to cook	who loves to dance
which is in Montana	where her horse is kept	that I like best
whom we chose for president	that we'll take soon	that we found

1. Forests (where) people camp should be left free of trash.
2. The car (that) I drove was candy-apple red.
3. My sister, (who) loves to dance, has a recital tonight.
4. This is the coach (whose) team won the game.
5. Tyler was the student (whom) we chose for president.
6. Michael showed us the restaurant (where) he works as a chef.
7. Ms. Gomez told us about the test, (that) we'll take soon.
8. The mountain, (which) is in Montana, is difficult to climb.
9. Maya visited the stables (where) her horse is kept.
10. My grandma is the one (who) taught me to cook.
11. California and Hawaii are two places (where) people surf.
12. Math, (which) is my best subject, is hard for some people.
13. Summer is the season (that) I like best.
14. The tigers (that) I read about are in danger of extinction.
15. The stray cats (that) we found all need good homes.

- **Now go back and circle the relative pronouns and subordinate conjunctions.**

Section 8.3

CHAPTER 6 Restrictive and Nonrestrictive Clauses

- **Underline the adjective clause in each sentence. Identify it as *restrictive* or *nonrestrictive* by writing *R* or *NR* on the line.**

1. Devon, who is a good athlete, made the football team. — NR
2. The oranges that you picked are in that basket. — R
3. Neena, who is new this year, went out for the tennis team. — NR
4. The kite that stuck in our tree is tangled in the leaves. — R
5. The eggs that dropped on the floor made a mess. — R
6. Yosemite, which is a large national park, is a favorite vacation spot. — NR
7. Thanksgiving, which falls on a Thursday, is an American holiday. — NR
8. Throw away the umbrella that won't open properly. — R
9. Several restaurants that she suggested sounded good. — R
10. The king, who had won the battle, finally returned home. — NR
11. The earrings that I bought are for my mom. — R
12. Yellow, which is my favorite color, brightens up a room. — NR

- **Circle the first letter of the noun described by each adjective phrase. Write the letters in order on the lines below. If your answers are correct, you will reveal the answer to the riddle.**

Name two keys that don't unlock doors.

Answer: d o n k e y and t u r k e y
       1 2 3 4 5 6   7 8 9 10 11 12

Section 8.4

CHAPTER 6 — Voice and Audience

- **Choose a word from the box to describe the voice and mood of each paragraph. Then list two phrases or sentences from the paragraph that set the tone.**

| angry | hopeful | enthusiastic | caring | concerned | funny |

Only $2,000 to go! Seaside Animal Shelter is holding a fund-raiser this weekend to raise money for our homeless and sick animals. We know, with your help, that we can do it! Come and join us for the bake sale, raffle, and games. With your participation, we will find each and every animal a loving home!

enthusiastic
Possible answer: We know we can do it. We will find each and every animal a loving home.

Our local government has decided to cut down the oak tree in Billows Park. We cannot let this happen! This tree has withstood the test of time. It has been a cherished symbol of our community for more than 200 years! Worst of all, the developer plans to build a huge, ugly condo complex at this site. Don't let the heart of this town be removed!

angry
Possible answer: worst of all, a huge, ugly condo complex

Mission Hospital has suddenly run short of its blood supply. We, the medical staff of Mission Hospital, implore everyone who is able to donate blood to do so at this weekend's blood drive. We should all be worried about this shortage. It's essential that we build up our reserve supply as soon as possible. This affects all of us. Please help us give you the best care possible.

concerned
Possible answer: suddenly run short, should all be worried

- **Rewrite the first paragraph so that it conveys a concerned voice and mood. Remember to choose vivid verbs, adjectives, and adverbs that will effectively convey the message to the reader.** Answers will vary.

CHAPTER 6 — Adverb Clauses

- **Underline the adverb clause in each sentence. Circle each subordinate conjunction.**

1. (Because) Jim was embarrassed, his face turned red.
2. (After) the game ended, we drove home.
3. I didn't know what to do (when) I missed the bus to school.
4. She will make the varsity team (if) she does well at the tryouts.
5. (While) Derek washed the car, Carla mowed the lawn.
6. The children acted (as if) they could stay awake all night.
7. We finished our homework (before) we went to the movie.
8. (Although) the water was cold, we enjoyed swimming in the river.
9. I will order the pizza (as soon as) the guests arrive.
10. The class cheered (when) Mr. Sanders postponed the test.

- **Write an adverb clause to complete each sentence.** Answers will vary.

11. Although _____, she still felt nervous during her performance.
12. When _____, I walked on the beach and went scuba diving.
13. You can improve your grades if _____.
14. Mom sliced the turkey while Dad _____.

Name _____ Date _____

CHAPTER 6 — Noun Clauses as Subjects

• Underline the noun clause used as a subject in each sentence. Circle the word that introduces each clause.

1. (That) Tia was the best singer in the group was not in question.
2. (Whatever) everyone decides to do is fine with me.
3. (Whether) I can afford the trip tops my list of concerns.
4. (That) we were so excited about the party caused my mother to smile.
5. (Whoever) baked these cupcakes deserves a blue ribbon!
6. (How) Tham finally won the race would make a wonderful story.
7. (Whomever) the coach decides to cut will be disappointed.
8. (That) we forgot to bring a gift caused us great embarrassment.

• Write a noun clause used as a subject to complete each sentence.
Answers will vary.

9. _____ may be considered my greatest talent.
10. _____ was obvious.
11. _____ has always fascinated me.
12. _____ is a good idea.

Section 8.6 • 93

Name _____ Date _____

CHAPTER 6 — Advertisements

• Identify the propaganda device used in each statement. Then use the same device to write a persuasive statement about the product named.

| bandwagon | loaded words | testimonial | vague or sweeping generalities |

1. Quarterback Jason Cooper claims, "Sore No More soothes all my aches and pains after a game!"
   testimonial
   Shampoo: **Sentences will vary.**

2. Give these cuddly, homeless kittens a safe, warm place to sleep at night.
   loaded words
   Zoo fundraiser: _____

3. No other store in the city can give you a better deal on a washing machine!
   vague or sweeping generalities
   Car dealership: _____

4. Even actress Shania Stone uses White 'n' Bright whitening toothpaste!
   testimonial
   Sports drink: _____

5. Everyone who's anyone loves Shakespeare in the Park!
   bandwagon
   Movie: _____

6. Jake's BBQ makes the spiciest baby back ribs in town!
   vague or sweeping generalities
   Summer carnival: _____

94 • Lesson 3

Name _____ Date _____

CHAPTER 6
Noun Clauses as Subject Complements

• Underline the noun clause used as a subject complement in each sentence. Circle the subject.

1. The best (solution) is that everyone brings food to share.
2. The main (problem) was that Jack decided to give up painting.
3. The (reason) remained that Jack wanted to study art in Europe.
4. The best (activity) might be when we all go swimming in the ocean.
5. My only (worry) is that you stay out too late without calling.
6. (Yoga) is what my sister studies at the recreation center.
7. The (question) now was who would take over after Jeffrey left.
8. My favorite (hour) is when the class goes outside to play softball.
9. The (fact) remains that Galileo improved a telescope developed by someone else.
10. Shane's (idea) is that we take our vacation in New Zealand.
11. Mom's favorite (vacation) was when Dad took her to Venice, Italy.
12. The best team (member) is whoever shows the most spirit.

• Now go back and circle the first letter of the subject in each even-numbered sentence. Write the letters in order on the lines below. If your answers are correct, you will reveal the answer to the riddle.

What is the best thing to do if a bull charges you?

Answer: __P__ __a__ __y__   __h__ __i__ __m__ !

Name _____ Date _____

CHAPTER 6
Noun Clauses as Appositives

• Underline the noun clause used as an appositive in each sentence. Circle the noun each clause renames.

1. The (theme) that hatred leads to tragedy is central to the play *Romeo and Juliet*.
2. The (tradition) that Romeo's and Juliet's families must fight does not keep the teenagers apart.
3. Romeo, however, maintains the (belief) that love will conquer all.
4. Juliet must hide the (fact) that she and Romeo were married in secret.
5. The friar has the (knowledge) that the marriage might be dangerous.
6. Juliet appears to be dead, so the (truth) that she took a sleeping potion isn't known immediately.
7. Unfortunately, Romeo believes the (rumor) that Juliet has died.
8. The (tragedy) that Romeo and Juliet both die at the end brings the families together.

• Find the nouns you circled in the word search. Words can go across, down, or diagonally.

```
T O T R I P B M A F
R N L H C W E H B A
U U S D E T L U N C
T H M U A M I K Y T
H K N O W L E D G E
C I R E S F I C T
  T R A D I T I O N L
W E T R A G E D Y S
```

CHAPTER 6 — Noun Clauses as Direct Objects

- **Underline the direct object in each sentence. Identify it as a *noun* or a *noun clause* by writing *N* or *NC*.**

1. Keisha realized <u>that she should have studied harder for the test</u>. **NC**
2. Most people take a <u>camera</u> when they go on vacation. **N**
3. We decided <u>that we would wait until noon to go to the beach</u>. **NC**
4. Ian asked <u>Bianca</u> for help in making the spaghetti dinner. **N**
5. Mateo wondered <u>how he could go out for two sports</u>. **NC**
6. My family discussed <u>how we would spend summer vacation</u>. **NC**
7. I'll choose <u>whatever looks best on me</u>. **NC**
8. Justin suggested the <u>idea</u> of painting the room green. **N**
9. Mom suggested <u>that we help her plant a vegetable garden</u>. **NC**
10. I wanted <u>flowers</u> rather than vegetables in the garden. **N**
11. Many people claimed <u>that they did not enjoy the movie</u>. **NC**
12. I prefer <u>movies</u> that are funny or about historical figures. **N**
13. Penny will perform <u>whichever is the best song for the show</u>. **NC**
14. Chelsea invited <u>whoever wanted to go to the party</u>. **NC**

CHAPTER 6 — Transition Words

- **Circle the transition word or phrase that correctly completes each sentence.**

1. Justin gave his speech to the audience, (while) in addition) Tera waited behind the curtain.
2. Katie held up the advertising sign (in front of) therefore) the new farmer's market.
3. All of us will make it to the game (but (unless) it starts to snow again.
4. Jennifer wouldn't enter her painting in the show (furthermore (because) she felt it wasn't good enough.
5. (However) Unlike), the books will continue to be on sale until Thursday.
6. Jamie wants to go to summer camp; (to begin with (on the other hand), he has an offer for a great part-time job.
7. The Strawberry Festival is lots of fun; (furthermore) therefore), it has the biggest Ferris wheel in the state.
8. (In addition) Before), the hospital needs more volunteers to help with patient care.
9. Bailey stored the boxes in the attic (unless (behind) Grandpa's big trunk.
10. Tyler practiced all summer long, (yet) while) he still didn't make the basketball team.

- **Use each transition word or phrase in a sentence. Answers will vary.**

11. (consequently) _____
12. (however) _____
13. (as a result) _____
14. (namely) _____

Name _____ Date _____

CHAPTER 6: Noun Clauses as Objects of Prepositions

• Underline the noun clause used as an object of a preposition in each sentence. Then circle the preposition that introduces each clause.

1. My friends talked (about) <u>what were the most violent kinds of storms</u>.
2. Jake told us (about) <u>what is known as the F-5 tornado</u>.
3. A tornado's power is ranked (by) <u>whatever its wind speed is</u>.
4. The F-5 is a tornado (with) <u>what are considered devastating winds</u>.
5. Most tornadoes occur (in) <u>what is known as the Midwest's Tornado Alley</u>.
6. In this area people learn (about) <u>how they can survive these storms</u>.
7. People tell frightening stories (about) <u>what they've seen during the storms</u>.
8. Warm, moist air is driven east (by) <u>what has developed into a cold front behind it</u>.

• Write a few sentences about a strange weather phenomenon you have experienced or read about. Include at least three noun clauses used as objects of prepositions in your writing. **Answers will vary.**

_____
_____
_____
_____
_____

Section 8.10 • 99

Name _____ Date _____

CHAPTER 6: Suffixes

• Add a suffix to each italicized word to create a new word that correctly completes the sentence. Write the new word on the line.

1. Some people want to *legal* a faster speed limit. — **legalize**
2. It is my *responsible* to take out the trash every night. — **responsibility**
3. After winning the writing contest, Maya felt *joy*. — **joyful or joyous**
4. Our class collected canned foods to donate to a *home* shelter. — **homeless**
5. Our teacher will *specific* which topics we need to study. — **specify**
6. My sister, Sara, wants to be a *paint* when she grows up. — **painter**
7. You will need to *active* the alarm before you leave. — **activate**
8. Cathy uses conditioner to *soft* her long, curly hair. — **soften**
9. Please ask Jake for some *assist* with these heavy boxes. — **assistance**
10. Jordan dropped *tired* onto the grass after the hike. — **tiredly**
11. The judge tried to settle their *disagree*. — **disagreement**
12. It was *thought* of him to show up late without calling. — **thoughtless**

• Look at the sample word analysis chart on page 138. Copy a blank chart on a separate sheet of paper. Complete the chart for the base word *help* to show how it changes with different suffixes. Use the suffixes *-less*, *-ful*, and *-er*. **Answers will vary.**

100 • Lesson 5

Name _____ Date _____

CHAPTER 6 — Simple, Compound, and Complex Sentences

• Write *simple*, *compound*, or *complex* on the lines below to identify each sentence type.

(1) Have you ever wondered about the formation of a rainbow? (2) It is actually quite simple. (3) When the conditions are right, sunlight passes through drops of water in the air. (4) Sunlight bends while passing through each drop, and the light separates into seven distinct colors. (5) If you want to see a rainbow, the sun must be behind you. (6) The water source must be in front of you. (7) The water source itself is not important; however, you will usually see rainbows after the rain. (8) You can see rainbows year-round, but you will see fewer of them during the winter. (9) Water drops in the air freeze more often in cold weather, and ice scatters light rather than bending it.

1. simple
2. simple
3. complex
4. compound
5. complex
6. simple
7. compound
8. compound
9. compound

• Use a simple, a compound, and a complex sentence to describe your favorite food, sport, friend, teacher, relative, or school subject. **Answers will vary.**

Simple: _____

Compound: _____

Complex: _____

Voyages in English 8 • Section 8.11 • 101

Name _____ Date _____

CHAPTER 6 — Self-Assessment

• Check *Always*, *Sometimes*, or *Never* to respond to each statement.

Writing

	Always	Sometimes	Never
I can identify the features of persuasive writing.			
I can identify and write for voice, mood, and audience.			
I can identify advertising and know how to write it.			
I can identify and use transition words.			
I can identify suffixes and use them to understand the meaning of a word.			
I include all the key features when I write a persuasive essay.			

Grammar

	Always	Sometimes	Never
I can identify and use declarative, interrogative, imperative, and exclamatory sentences.			
I can identify and use adjective and adverb phrases.			
I can identify and use adjective clauses.			
I can identify and use restrictive and nonrestrictive clauses.			
I can identify and use adverb clauses.			
I can identify and use noun clauses as subjects.			
I can identify and use noun clauses as subject complements.			
I can identify and use noun clauses as appositives.			
I can identify and use noun clauses as direct objects.			
I can identify and use noun clauses as objects of prepositions.			
I can identify and use simple, compound, and complex sentences.			

• Write the most helpful thing you learned in this chapter.

_____

102 • Chapter 6 Self-Assessment • Voyages in English 8

Name _____ Date _____

CHAPTER 7 — Coordinating Conjunctions

- Circle the correct coordinating conjunction to complete each sentence. Then identify what the conjunction joins by writing *words*, *phrases*, or *clauses*.

1. Bailey couldn't decide between pizza (**and** / or) spaghetti. — **words**
2. I tried to hear the speech, (**but** / nor) the crowd was too noisy. — **clauses**
3. Cameron double-majored in English (or / **and**) in biology. — **phrases**
4. Should I take a plane (for / **or**) a train to get to Chicago? — **words**
5. The theater was crowded, (or / **yet**) I could still see everything. — **clauses**
6. We took the long (for / **but**) beautiful trail to the mountaintop. — **words**
7. Jenna planned to ski (**and** / but) to get some rest. — **phrases**
8. We will not travel to Spain, (and / **nor**) will we go to Italy. — **clauses**
9. We can paint the room baby blue (so / **or**) lemon yellow. — **words**
10. It is raining outside, (**so** / for) we won't go to the beach. — **clauses**
11. We can't get into the museum today, (**but** / so) we can return tomorrow. — **clauses**
12. Kayla couldn't find her cat, (but / **nor**) did she have any idea where it might have gone. — **clauses**

- Write two sentences using coordinating conjunctions. Then circle each conjunction and identify what it joins by writing *words*, *phrases*, or *clauses*. **Answers will vary.**

13. _____

14. _____

Name _____ Date _____

CHAPTER 7 — Correlative Conjunctions

- Circle the correlative conjunctions in each sentence. If the sentence does not have correlative conjunctions, write *none* after the sentence.

1. Jason is buying (**not only**) the baseballs (**but also**) the bats and mitts.
2. (**Either**) Mindy (**or**) Mom will make the cake.
3. Would you like to play games or to go swimming? **none**
4. (**Neither**) Lisa (**nor**) Eric can make it to class on time.
5. (**Whether**) a puppy (**or**) a kitten, Annie wants a pet.
6. Lexi and her sister are both making cookies for the party. **none**
7. (**Both**) Michael (**and**) I will run in the marathon on Saturday.
8. Bianca (**not only**) acted in the play (**but also**) sang.
9. In case I am late, we can meet at (**either**) the restaurant (**or**) the museum.
10. Terrance will drive (**neither**) the truck (**nor**) the van.
11. Let's bring corn and chicken to the neighborhood picnic. **none**
12. (**Whether**) Shana will play the leading role (**or**) be the director's assistant is still undecided.

- Write two sentences about school. Include correlative conjunctions in each sentence and circle them. **Answers will vary.**

13. _____

14. _____

Name _____ Date _____

CHAPTER 7 — What Makes Good Playwriting?

- **Read this excerpt from a play. Then answer the questions below.**

HANNAH: *(straggling behind the others)* This is crazy, you guys. It's a myth, a legend.
MATT: *(turning to face Hannah)* Then why are you here? You have doubted this story all along and yet here you are, right beside us.
ANDY: *(kneels between the rock and boulder)* I think it's here. Look. *(unfolds a tattered piece of paper for friends to examine)*
TERRI: The map shows a tree and a rock just like this!
HANNAH: Oh, sure. This is the only rock and tree around here.
MATT: Just ignore her. Let's see if our detective work has paid off. *(Hannah retreats to downstage right where she busies herself plucking grass. The other three children begin digging. There is a metallic clink as one of the children's shovels makes contact with an object. The three children kneel beside the hole.)*
ANDY: *(awestruck)* Wow!
(Hannah gets to her feet and peers at the others from a distance.)
TERRI: Well, we never expected that, did we?
MATT: Hannah, of all of us, you really need to see this!

1. What is most likely the setting for this play? What details lead to that conclusion?
   A scene outdoors, perhaps a meadow or the edge of a woods; The stage directions mention a rock and a boulder. The children are digging near a rock and a tree.

2. Would this scene most likely occur in the beginning, middle, or end of the play? Explain your answer.
   Possibly the end because they have been doing detective work and are about to reveal a discovery

3. Consider Hannah. What do you know about this character based on the details provided in the script?
   Hannah is doubtful and doesn't believe in legends. She is curious though and tags along anyway.

Lesson 1 • 105

Name _____ Date _____

CHAPTER 7 — Conjunctive Adverbs

- **Circle the conjunctive adverb or parenthetical expression that correctly completes each sentence.**

1. There is only one cookie left; (**however**, besides), Mom is making more.
2. Dad is firing up the barbecue; (**therefore**, finally), we should buy some steaks.
3. Pizza is a spicy, delicious food; (later, **moreover**), it's pretty good for you!
4. I didn't plant enough peas; (then, **in fact**), I didn't plant enough beans either.
5. The horse is not fully trained; (however, **consequently**), it's not ready for the show.
6. Jackson built an extra bedroom; (later, **still**), it became his home office.
7. Luke must paint the playhouse soon; (finally, **otherwise**), the children will be too big to play in it.
8. Min chose a college close to home; (**thus**, besides), she'll be home on weekends.
9. Finals were finished today; (besides, **finally**), summer has arrived!
10. Our house is in the mountains; (**indeed**, thus), it sits on a peak over 5,000 feet above sea level.
11. Fashion is very important to Kate; (nonetheless, **likewise**), it is the main interest of her twin sister.
12. The county fair has great food; (**furthermore**, still), it provides wonderful entertainment.
13. Kaley would like to join the tennis team; (**on the other hand**, therefore), she is an outstanding volleyball player.
14. The lake is too deep for swimming; (nevertheless, **besides**), it's too cold outside.

106 • Section 9.3

Name _____ Date _____

CHAPTER 7

Subordinate Conjunctions

- **Circle each subordinate conjunction and underline the dependent clauses. Not every sentence has a subordinate conjunction.**

Jackie Robinson was the first African American to play in the American professional baseball leagues. Before that time African Americans played in the Negro Leagues. (When) Robinson signed his contract with the Brooklyn Dodgers in 1945, he broke the "color barrier." (As long as) this barrier existed, sports would continue to have teams based on color. Robinson rose to the challenge. (Although) he dealt with racism on a daily basis, Robinson showed great courage and persistence. He proved to everyone that he belonged in the majors. In 1946 and 1947 Robinson won the National League batting title. He triumphed again in 1949, (when) he was named the league's most valuable player. Robinson set many team and league records (as) he played out his career with the Dodgers.

- **Write a few sentences about a favorite sports hero or other famous person. Use at least three subordinate conjunctions in your writing.**
Answers will vary.

Name _____ Date _____

CHAPTER 7

Play Structure and Format

- **Read this excerpt from a short story. Use what you know about play structure and format to rewrite this excerpt as part of a script. Be creative as you develop the setting and character descriptions. Use underlining instead of italics to designate stage directions and other details that are not spoken.**

Sarah Jane sighed as she watched the sun set beyond the hills. She turned from the doorway, lit the kerosene lamp on the table, and sat down, adjusting her long skirts about her. At last, Sarah Jane spoke. "Why are you here, Mr. Corteney?"

"I've come to inquire about your father's accounts. They are overdue," replied the thin, dour man. He reminded Sarah Jane of an undertaker.

"As I told you before, my father is not here. He is away . . ."

"Seeking his fortune at the silver mines," interrupted Mr. Corteney. "Yes, you told me. But it has been too long, my dear. I cannot extend you credit forever."

Sarah Jane brushed a lock of red hair from her eyes. "I understand, sir. But I can do nothing myself. Father promised he would return by May, in two months' time. Surely waiting two months is better than receiving no money at all."

Mr. Corteney stood up, gathering his hat and cane. "All right," he replied. "I will return, but make no mistake, Miss Sarah Jane. I must be paid at that time, with money or with your farm. The decision will be yours."

He left, slamming the door behind him, and leaving Sarah Jane absorbed in thought.

Answers will vary.

Name _____ Date _____

CHAPTER 7 Troublesome Conjunctions

- Write the conjunction or the preposition that correctly completes each sentence. Use the words in the box.

without	unless	like	as if	as

1. Justin found it difficult to see the board **without** his glasses.
2. **Unless** you put on this coat, you will get wet in the rain.
3. Elena looks **as if** she has been up all night studying.
4. No one should go outside in the snow **without** boots.
5. That lion looks **like** my cat.
6. We sent a small gift **as** a special thank-you to our coach.
7. Does this candy taste **like** watermelon?
8. **Without** an excuse from the doctor, you will be marked absent.
9. Shari ran **as if** she were being chased by wild horses.
10. I held on to my hat **as** the wind whipped around me.
11. Please don't walk after dark **unless** you have a friend with you.
12. My mom's chocolate cake is **like** no one else's.
13. Jim acted **as if** he had won the top prize.

- Complete each sentence. *Answers will vary.*

14. I look a lot like _____.
15. I can't go one day without _____.

Section 9.5 • 109

Name _____ Date _____

CHAPTER 7 Interjections

- Underline the interjection in each sentence. Then write another sentence using the same interjection. You may set it off from the rest of the sentence, or use it as part of an exclamatory sentence.

1. <u>Oh no</u>, the rain is really pouring down!
   Sentences will vary.
2. <u>Ouch</u>! I hit my knee on the corner of the coffee table.
3. <u>Hush</u>! The baby is sleeping.
4. <u>Hooray</u>, they scored another touchdown!
5. <u>No</u>! Don't chew on those slippers.
6. <u>Wow</u>, that show was amazing!
7. <u>Yes</u>, I would love to go ice skating!
8. <u>Hey</u>! Please move your car out of the way.

- On another sheet of paper, illustrate one of the sentences above to show the emotion the interjection conveys. Put the interjection in a speech bubble. *Drawings will vary.*

110 • Section 9.6

CHAPTER 7: Dialog, Monolog, and Asides

- **Read the scene description. Write dialog to develop the scene and characters. Include a monolog and an aside.**

> Sanji is planning a surprise party for her best friend, Rachel, and she is determined to keep it a surprise. Sanji's pesky younger brother, James, however, tricks her into giving up the secret in front of Rachel one rainy afternoon.

Answers will vary, but students should include an example of an aside and a monolog that fits within the context of the dialog.

CHAPTER 7: Punctuation—Part I

- **Rewrite each sentence, adding or taking out punctuation as necessary.**

1. Mrs Davis asked "How many, students want to go on the field trip?"
   Mrs. Davis asked, "How many students want to go on the field trip?"

2. Shane my little brother was born on, Monday June 7 2004 at lunchtime.
   Shane, my little brother, was born on Monday, June 7, 2004, at lunchtime.

3. Many people love New York New York and I am one of them
   Many people love New York, New York, and I am one of them.

4. "Sir you forgot your coat" Tanya told Mr Chang
   "Sir, you forgot your coat," Tanya told Mr. Chang.

5. I can't decide whether to visit San Diego California or Dallas Texas
   I can't decide whether to visit San Diego, California, or Dallas, Texas.

6. Alana Sam and, Trey placed first, second and third, so I heard in the spelling bee
   Alana, Sam, and Trey placed first, second, and third, so I heard, in the spelling bee.

7. "I need" Dad continued "some help with these dishes"
   "I need," Dad continued, "some help with these dishes."

8. His full name which is known only to his friends is Charles S Winslow III
   His full name, which is known only to his friends, is Charles S. Winslow III.

9. Collene the guests are beginning to arrive
   Collene, the guests are beginning to arrive.

10. The children were tired yet they did not want to go to sleep
    The children were tired, yet they did not want to go to sleep.

Name _____ Date _____

CHAPTER 7
Idioms, Slang, and Jargon

• Use an example of idioms, slang, or jargon from the box to complete each line of dialog. Each sentence comes from a different play, so use the context of the dialog within the item to figure out your answer.

boom swings over the aft deck	lend a hand	in over your head
rubbed him the wrong way	mellow out	ollie that four-set
see eye to eye	sit tight	

1. PERCIVAL: *(disgustedly)* I thought you were my biggest supporter, but now I can understand that we no longer **see eye to eye**.

2. MOTHER: *(turns to Dora)* Here, let me **lend a hand**. The task will not be such a chore with both of us doing it.

3. CAPTAIN: *(shouts loudly)* Comin' about. Look alive, mates. Mind your skulls as the **boom swings over the aft deck**.

4. PROFESSOR: *(pompously)* Are you sure medicine is the right degree for you? You failed your midterm exam, and your lab results are less than satisfactory. I do believe you are **in over your head**.

5. HIPPIE: Hey, **mellow out**. Me and my ol' lady see how uptight you are, man.

6. LT. NELSON: Men, **sit tight** while I scout over the next bluff. Count to 20, then charge over the bluff with everything you've got.

7. BUD: *(in disbelief)* Did you see the way Rudy looked at me? Wow, somehow I must have **rubbed him the wrong way**.

8. MATT: *(strips off his helmet)* I thought I could **ollie that four-set**, but I had to bail off board at the last minute.

• Choose one of the script lines above. With a classmate, write and act out a short dialog that incorporates the line.

114 • Lesson 4

Name _____ Date _____

CHAPTER 7
Punctuation— Part II

• Rewrite the paragraph, adding or taking out punctuation as necessary.

Hooray Finally summer had arrived. All year I had been planning a list of things to do go camping with friends, visit my grandparents in Minnesota, repair my bike; and get a part-time job. I couldn't wait to get started however, I didn't know what to do first. Should I visit my grandparents. Should I look for a job! I thought I might work at an animal shelter, namely, Animal Avenue, where my best friend volunteers. I could work early in the morning the rest of the day would be free. Yes. This was going to be the best summer ever.

Possible answer: **Hooray! Finally summer had arrived. All year I had been planning a list of things to do: go camping with friends, visit my grandparents in Minnesota, repair my bike, and get a part-time job. I couldn't wait to get started; however, I didn't know what to do first. Should I visit my grandparents? Should I look for a job? I thought I might work at an animal shelter; namely, Animal Avenue, where my best friend volunteers. I could work early in the morning; the rest of the day would be free. Yes! This was going to be the best summer ever.**

• Rewrite the following sentences with the correct punctuation.

1. We visited several countries namely France Germany and Spain
   We visited several countries; namely, France, Germany, and Spain.

2. These are the chores I'd like you to do clean your room feed the pets and mow the lawn
   These are the chores I'd like you to do: clean your room, feed the pets, and mow the lawn.

3. Wow that game was exciting
   Possible answer: Wow, that game was exciting! or Wow! That game was exciting.

4. Did you remember to bring your raincoat
   Did you remember to bring your raincoat?

5. Brian carried the boxes upstairs they were very heavy
   Brian carried the boxes upstairs; they were very heavy.

Section 10.2 • 113

CHAPTER 7

Punctuation—Part III

• Rewrite each sentence using quotation marks and italics. Use underlining to indicate italics.

1. Did you read this article in today's L.A. Times? Dad asked.
   "Did you read this article in today's *L.A. Times*?" Dad asked.

2. Please, my little sister begged, let me go with you to the mall.
   "Please," my little sister begged, "let me go with you to the mall."

3. The book Renaissance Artists shows a picture of da Vinci's painting The Last Supper.
   The book *Renaissance Artists* shows a picture of da Vinci's painting *The Last Supper*.

4. Have you read the story Lost in Memphis? my teacher asked.
   "Have you read the story 'Lost in Memphis'?" my teacher asked.

5. You can find the article Tennis Legends in this month's Sports Illustrated for Kids.
   You can find the article "Tennis Legends" in this month's *Sports Illustrated for Kids*.

6. This story, Mr. Loomis said, is based on the poem Among the Leaves.
   "This story," Mr. Loomis said, "is based on the poem 'Among the Leaves.'"

7. The lyrics for The Star-Spangled Banner can be found in American Songbook.
   The lyrics for "The Star-Spangled Banner" can be found in *American Songbook*.

8. Did you see the movie To Touch the Sky: Climbing Mt. Everest last summer?
   Did you see the movie *To Touch the Sky: Climbing Mt. Everest* last summer?

9. The Queen Elizabeth 2 is one of the world's largest passenger ships.
   The *Queen Elizabeth 2* is one of the world's largest passenger ships.

10. Amazing Animal Rescues is my favorite television show! exclaimed Troy.
    "*Amazing Animal Rescues* is my favorite television show!" exclaimed Troy.

CHAPTER 7

Punctuation—Part IV

• Fill in the circle in front of the answer that shows the correct punctuation.

1. The Smiths dog
   ○ The Smith's dog
   ○ The Smiths dog's
   ● The Smiths' dog

2. Words with us and os
   ○ Words with us' and os'
   ● Words with *u*'s and *o*'s
   ○ Words with *us* and *os*

3. Twenty five years worth
   ○ Twenty-five year's worth
   ● Twenty-five years' worth
   ○ Twenty-five years's worth

4. Sixth graders graduation
   ○ Sixth-graders graduation
   ● Sixth-graders' graduation
   ○ Sixth grader's graduation

5. Im in the class of 06
   ● I'm in the class of '06
   ○ I'm in the class of 06
   ○ I'm in the class of "06"

6. My mother in laws purse
   ○ My mother-in laws' purse
   ● My mother's-in-law purse
   ○ My mother-in-law's purse

7. The forty two cats of the Jones family
   ○ The Jone's fortytwo cats
   ● The Joneses' forty-two cats
   ○ The Jones' forty-two cats

8. The Unions flag in 63
   ○ The Unions flag in "63"
   ○ The Unions flag in '63
   ● The Union's flag in '63

9. Shes a nine year old girl
   ○ Shes a nine-year-old-girl
   ● She's a nine-year-old girl
   ○ She's a nine year old girl

• Rewrite each sentence using apostrophes, hyphens, and dashes correctly.

10. I invited both sisters in law I'm so glad they get along to dinner.
    I invited both sisters-in-law—I'm so glad they get along—to dinner.

11. Well never forget our high schools ten year reunion.
    We'll never forget our high school's ten-year reunion.

12. The childrens first aid kit we found it under the sink really came in handy.
    The children's first-aid kit—we found it under the sink—really came in handy.

CHAPTER 7 Free Verse

- **Write interesting words or phrases that express each abstract word. Answers will vary.**

  1. exhaustion _____
  2. satisfaction _____
  3. accomplishment _____
  4. tenderness _____
  5. joy _____

- **Read the prose passage below. Think about how you could use the information to write a free-verse poem. On a separate sheet of paper, use a word/idea web to brainstorm figurative or sensory language or rhyming words you could use in your poem. For an example of a word/idea web, see page 137. Then write your free-verse poem on the lines below. Answers will vary.**

Dew is a deposit of water drops that forms at night when water vapor in the air condenses on the surfaces of objects. Dew forms on clear, still nights. This is because exposed surfaces, such as leaves, blades of grass, and petals lose heat to the atmosphere by radiation at a rate much faster than the surrounding air. These surfaces become cooler than the air and cause any water vapor in the air to condense on the surfaces. The resulting dew appears as tiny beads of water on plant parts.

CHAPTER 7 Capital Letters

- **Rewrite each paragraph using correct capitalization.**

my favorite book is *little house on the prairie* by laura ingalls wilder. while reading the book, I learned a lot about what life was like in america long ago. I was interested to learn how the ingalls family survived on the Prairie. My favorite part was when they met the native americans. I read the book as an english assignment, but now I have read almost the whole Series. i think I will be finished by june, right before Summer.

My favorite book is *Little House on the Prairie* by Laura Ingalls Wilder. While reading the book, I learned a lot about what life was like in America long ago. I was interested to learn how the Ingalls family survived on the prairie. My favorite part was when they met the Native Americans. I read the book as an English assignment, but now I have read almost the whole series. I think I will be finished by June, right before summer.

dr. steinberg is the best veterinarian I know. she graduated from the university of california at davis, the same college uncle troy attended. dr. steinberg treated all of our animals, including my dog happy and my hamster fred. i was very sad when she told me she was moving to tulsa, oklahoma, to be near her family. dr. steinberg will be opening her own practice there called the precious pets clinic.

Dr. Steinberg is the best veterinarian I know. She graduated from the University of California at Davis, the same college Uncle Troy attended. Dr. Steinberg treated all of our animals, including my dog Happy and my hamster Fred. I was very sad when she told me she was moving to Tulsa, Oklahoma, to be near her family. Dr. Steinberg will be opening her own practice there called The Precious Pets Clinic.

CHAPTER 7 Self-Assessment

- Check *Always, Sometimes,* or *Never* to respond to each statement.

Writing

	Always	Sometimes	Never
I can identify the features of playwriting.			
I can identify the structure and format of a play, including character and setting descriptions, dialog, and stage directions.			
I can identify and write dialog, monologs, and asides.			
I can identify and use idioms, slang, and jargon.			
I can identify the features of free verse.			
I include all the key features when I write a scene for a play.			

Grammar

	Always	Sometimes	Never
I can identify and use coordinating conjunctions.			
I can identify and use correlative conjunctions.			
I can identify and use conjunctive adverbs.			
I can identify and use subordinate conjunctions.			
I can identify troublesome conjunctions and use them correctly.			
I can identify and use interjections.			
I can identify and use periods and commas.			
I can identify and use semicolons, colons, exclamation points, and question marks.			
I can identify and use quotation marks, italics, and underlining.			
I can identify and use apostrophes, hyphens, and dashes.			
I can identify and use capital letters.			

- What was your favorite part of this chapter? Write an explanation on the lines.

_____

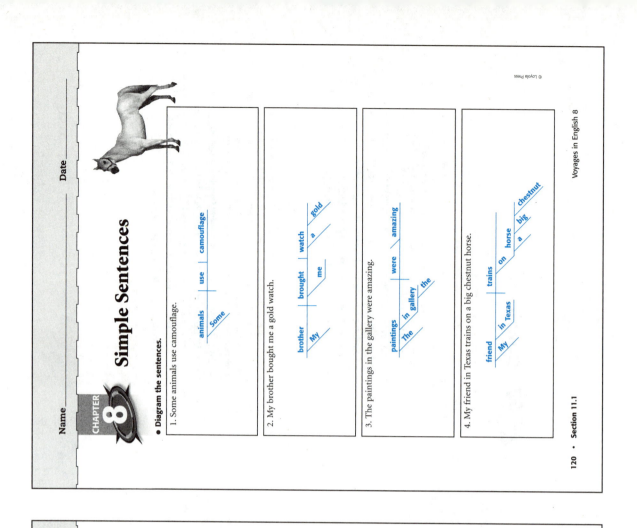

CHAPTER 8 Simple Sentences

- Diagram the sentences.

1. Some animals use camouflage.

2. My brother bought me a gold watch.

3. The paintings in the gallery were amazing.

4. My friend in Texas trains on a big chestnut horse.

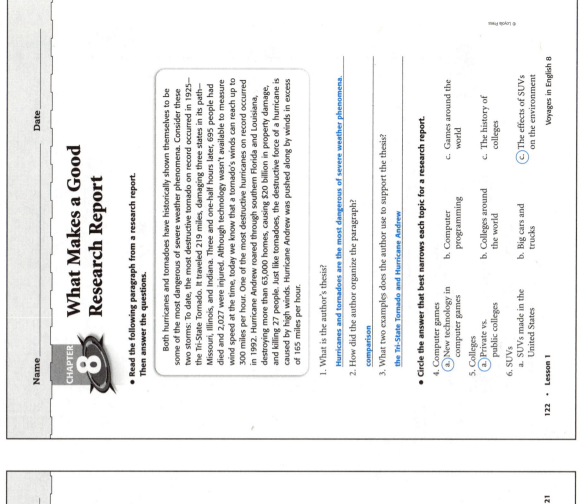

Chapter 8: Compound Sentence Elements

- Diagram the sentences.

1. Sara and I planted tomatoes in the vegetable garden.
2. Dylan sketched and painted pictures for the art fair.
3. My best friend and I watched movies and played board games.
4. My mother is intelligent and beautiful.

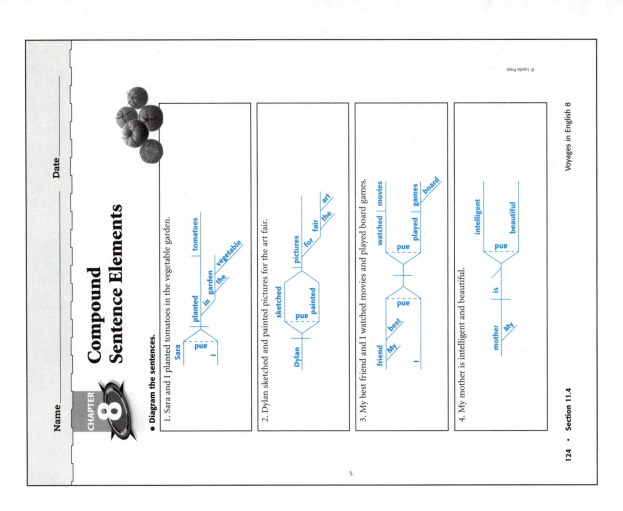

Chapter 8: Compound Sentences

- Diagram the sentences.

1. I brought my backpack; however, I forgot my camera.
2. Justin ate four hot dogs; afterwards, he had two pieces of pie.
3. The rain poured down on us, but we finished the baseball game.
4. Shari majored in English; in fact, she has two degrees in modern literature.

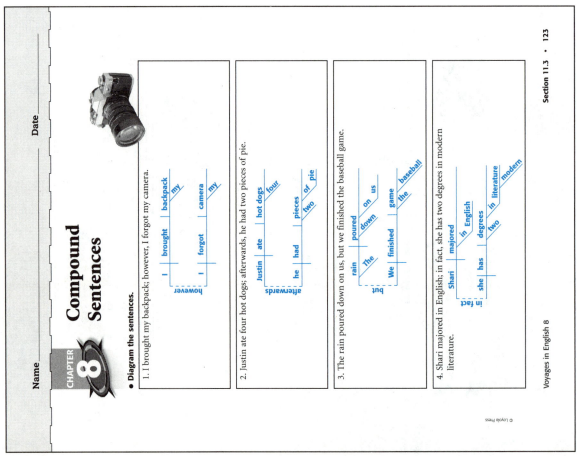

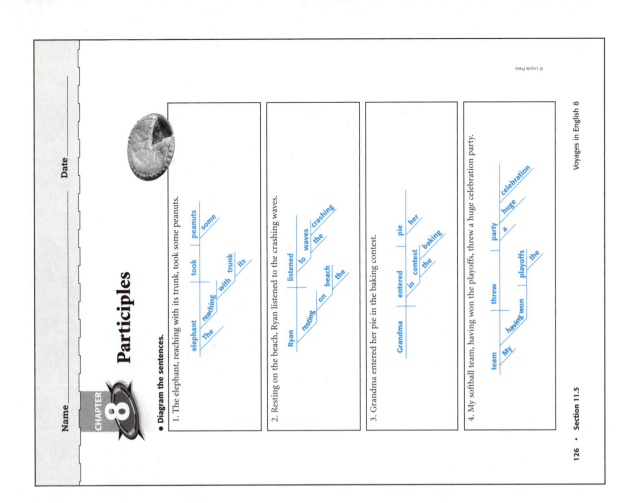

Chapter 8: Gerunds

Diagram the sentences.

1. Playing tennis is my best skill.
2. My dad enjoys watching old movies.
3. Some dogs are trained for leading the blind.
4. My new hobby, flying kites, is great on a windy spring day.

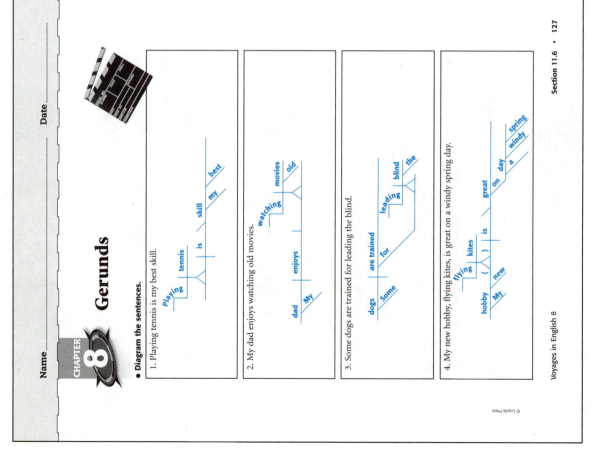

Chapter 8: Citing Sources

Write the citation for each source.

1. Book Title: Seasons in Change
   City and State of Publisher: New York, NY
   Author: Tyler Small, Publication Year: 2002
   Publisher: In Print Publishing

2. Magazine Title: Computer Expert
   Pages of Article: 33–37
   Publication Date: June 8, 2000
   Article Title: Watch Out! New Viruses
   Authors: James Walker, Lin Nguyn

3. Interviewee's Name: Justin Krall
   Date of Interview: May 12, 2004

4. TV Program Title: Mars: The Red Planet
   Date Aired: December 6, 2003
   Network: Explorer Channel
   Network City & State: Dallas, Texas

5. Web Site Name: School Days
   Author: Shane L. Thomas
   Document Title: Making Math Easy
   Web Site Address: www.schooldays.org
   Date Accessed: August 10, 2004

6. Encyclopedia Name: Encyclopaedia Brittanica
   Edition Year: 1999
   Article Title: The American Revolution

7. Newspaper Title: Chicago Journal
   Authors: Cherise Jones, Maggie Wright
   Pages of Article: 3–5
   Publication Date: January 22, 2001
   Article Title: Voting on Election Day

8. Book Title: The General: George Washington
   Publication Year: 1992
   Publisher: WordWorks, Inc.
   Author: Elena Ana Lopez
   City and State of Publisher: Chicago, IL

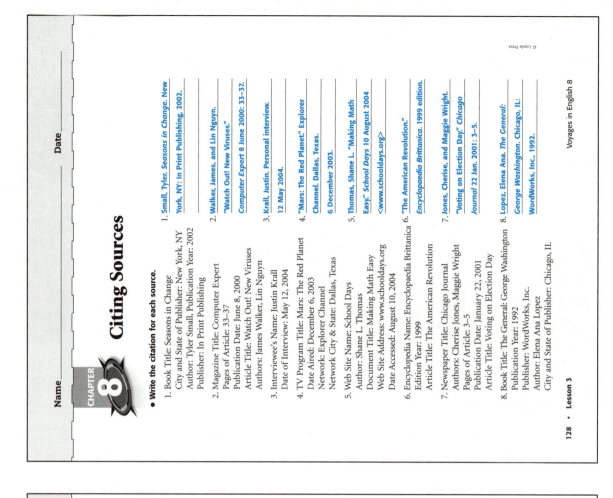

1. Small, Tyler. *Seasons in Change.* New York, NY: In Print Publishing, 2002.

2. Walker, James, and Lin Nguyn. "Watch Out! New Viruses." *Computer Expert* 8 June 2000: 33–37.

3. Krall, Justin. Personal interview. 12 May 2004.

4. "Mars: The Red Planet." Explorer Channel. Dallas, Texas. 6 December 2003.

5. Thomas, Shane L. "Making Math Easy." *School Days* 10 August 2004 <www.schooldays.org>

6. "The American Revolution." *Encyclopaedia Brittanica.* 1999 edition.

7. Jones, Cherise, and Maggie Wright. "Voting on Election Day." *Chicago Journal* 22 Jan. 2001: 3–5.

8. Lopez, Elena Ana. *The General: George Washington.* Chicago, IL: WordWorks, Inc, 1992.

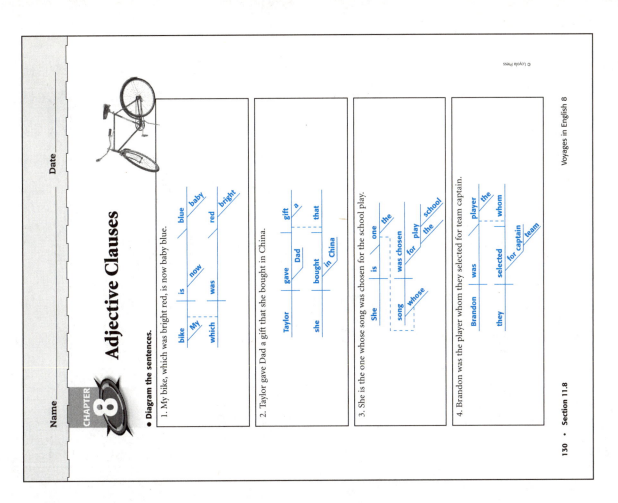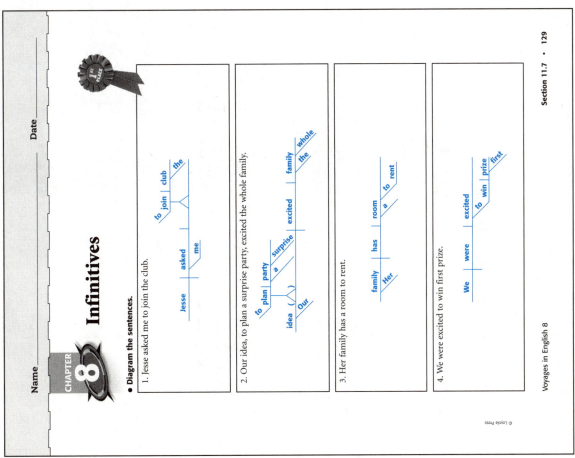

CHAPTER 8 Reference Tools

- Identify the research tool you would use to find information about each topic. Some items may have more than one answer.

| encyclopedia | almanac | bibliographical reference |
| catalog | atlas | Reader's Guide to Periodical Literature |

1. The top songs of 1997   almanac
2. A book about the legend of King Arthur   bibliographical reference
3. The history of movies in the United States   *Reader's Guide to Periodical Literature*
4. The life of Dr. Martin Luther King Jr.   encyclopedia, bibliographical reference
5. Annual rainfall numbers for Arizona   almanac
6. Magazine articles on Italian cooking   *Reader's Guide to Periodical Literature*
7. A book about raising Siamese cats   catalog
8. Mountainous regions in Argentina   atlas
9. The American Revolution   bibliographical reference
10. The basketball career of Michael Jordan   biographical reference, encyclopedia
11. Articles on general car maintenance   catalog
12. The political boundaries of Poland   atlas
13. Famous scientists of the 20th century   bibliographical reference
14. Pulitzer Prize winners   almanac, encyclopedia
15. Magazine articles on Olympic diving   *Reader's Guide to Periodical Literature*

CHAPTER 8 Adverb Clauses

- Diagram the sentences.

1. Since Keisha joined our class, discussions are much more interesting.

2. Although Carter loves the rain, he is afraid of thunderstorms.

3. We will show the slides when Lisa returns from her vacation.

4. The nature group hiked up the mountain before the sun went down.

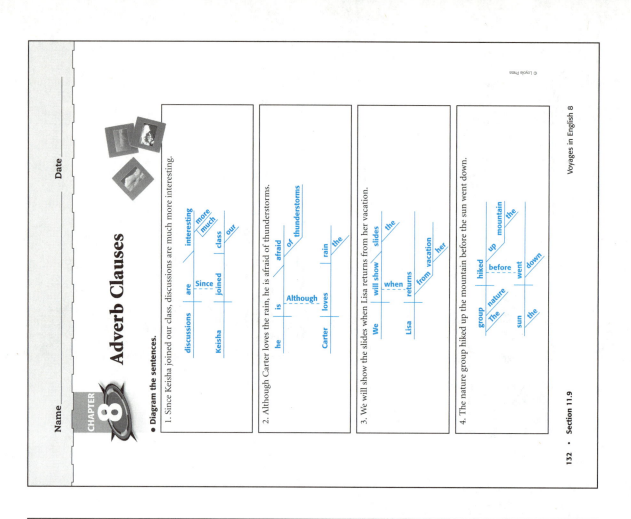

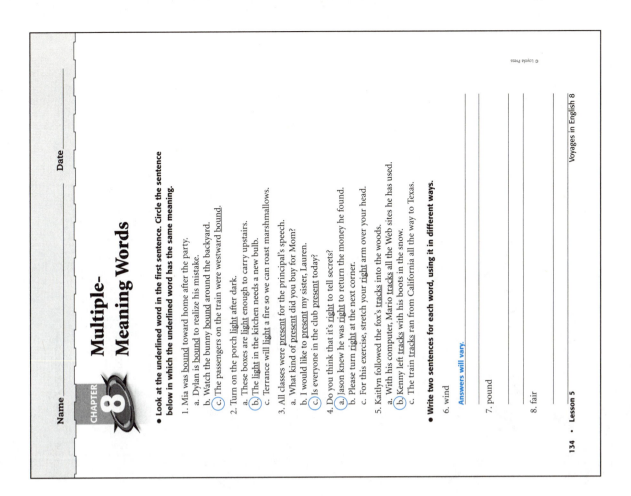

Practice Book Answers • 71

Name _____ Date _____

CHAPTER 8 Self-Assessment

• Check *Always*, *Sometimes*, or *Never* to respond to each statement.

Writing	Always	Sometimes	Never
I can identify the features of a research report.			
I can take effective notes and organize an outline.			
I can identify and cite sources.			
I can identify and use reference tools.			
I can identify multiple-meaning words and use them correctly.			
I include all the key features when I write a research report.			

Grammar	Always	Sometimes	Never
I can diagram simple sentences.			
I can diagram sentences with appositives.			
I can diagram compound sentences.			
I can diagram compound elements in sentences.			
I can diagram sentences with participles.			
I can diagram sentences with gerunds.			
I can diagram sentences with infinitives.			
I can diagram sentences with adjective and adverb clauses.			
I can diagram sentences with noun clauses.			

• Explain how learning to diagram a sentence will help you be a better writer.

_____
_____
_____

Name _____ Date _____

CHAPTER 8 Diagramming Review

• Diagram the sentences.

1. Kendra and Luke tried to stop, but their sled crashed into the snow bank.

2. My brother Aaron and his friend climbed Mt. Whitney and hiked the Pacific Coast Trail to Washington.

3. The golden lion, roaring with all its might, rushed at its unsuspecting prey.

4. Dr. Phillips, who treats all my animals, asked me to help with the new pet adoption program.

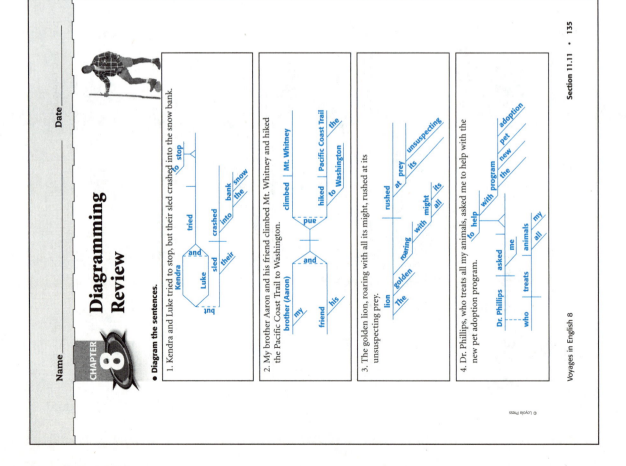

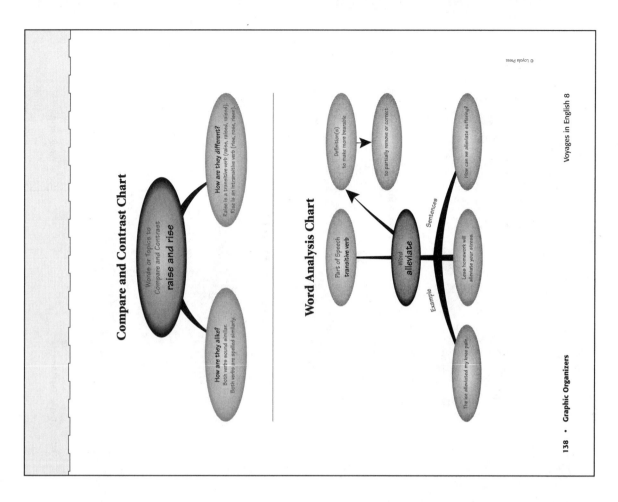

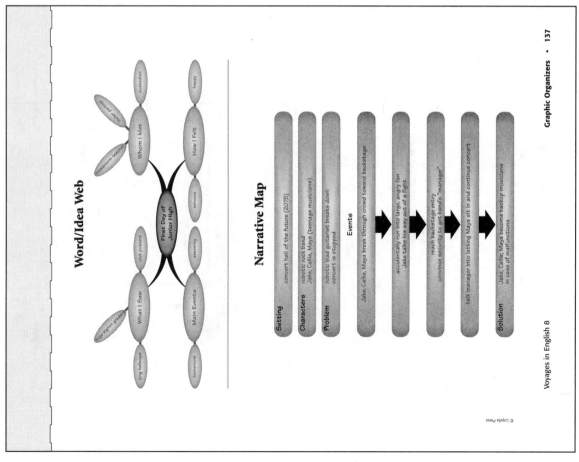

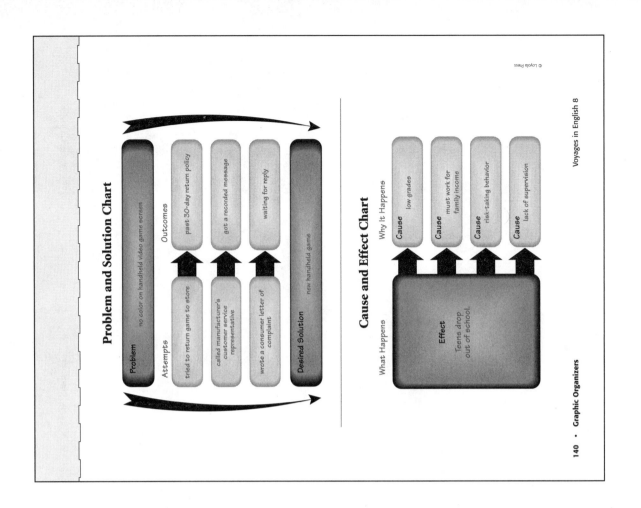

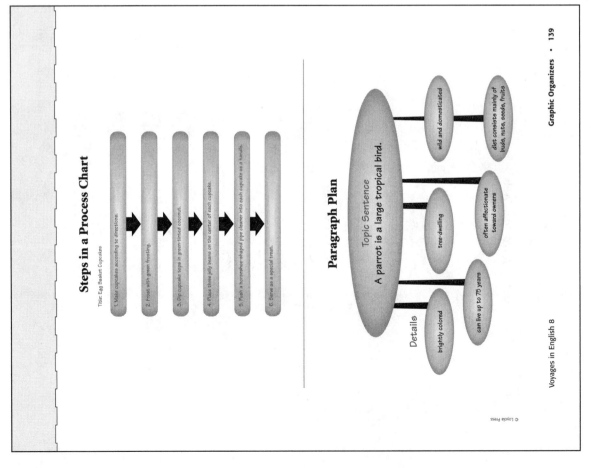

Assessment Book
Answer Key

VOYAGES
IN ENGLISH
Writing and Grammar

8

How the Assessment Books Work

The Assessment Book provides teachers with a variety of ways to assess how their students are doing. Each chapter begins with a two-page Pre-test, for assessing students' current level of understanding, and ends with a two-page Post-test, for evaluating students' mastery of the concepts. A two-page lesson, Test Preparation, introduces students to the types of questions and subjects they will encounter on standardized tests. The Student's Genre Writing Prompt and Genre Scoring Rubric gives students the opportunity to assess their own writing skills.

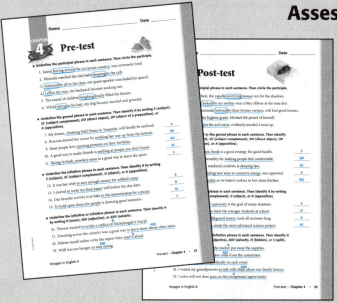

Assessment Book Rubrics

Chapter Pre-tests and Post-tests (two pages each) give teachers the information they need to plan the curriculum and to assess what students have learned.

A standardized-format Genre Writing Prompt and a Student's Genre Scoring Rubric allow students to self-assess their writing skills.

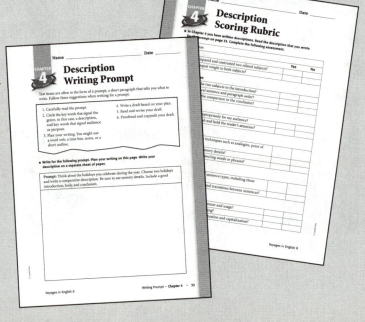

CHAPTER 1 Pre-test

Name _____ Date _____

● **Write the possessive form of the first noun in parentheses and the plural form of the second noun in parentheses. Then underline count nouns once and noncount nouns twice.**

1. (Mr. Jones) __Mr. Jones's__ class is keeping (mouse) __mice__ as mascots.
2. This is (Trey) __Trey's__ first time donating (blood) __blood__.
3. Inside the (valley) __valley's__ mountains lie gold and (silver) __silver__.
4. (Jamie and Tom) __Jamie and Tom's__ brother has surfed along the California (beach) __beaches__.
5. Half of (Grandpa) __Grandpa's__ garden contains beans and (potato) __potatoes__.

● **Identify the use of the underlined nouns in each sentence. Write S (subject), SC (subject complement), ID (indirect object), or OC (object complement).**

6. __S, SC__ My <u>house</u> is the largest single-family <u>residence</u> on our street.
7. __S, ID__ Ms. <u>Jenkins</u> gave her <u>students</u> an extra credit assignment.
8. __S, OC__ The football <u>team</u> elected Paco <u>captain</u> for the year.
9. __ID, OC__ We bought Sean a <u>puppy</u>, which he named <u>Buddy</u>.
10. __S, ID__ <u>Charles</u> sent his <u>girlfriend</u> one dozen pink roses.

● **Underline the adjective phrase or clause in each sentence. Identify it by writing P (phrase) or C (clause) on the line. Then circle the correct descriptive, comparative, or superlative adjective to complete each sentence.**

11. __C__ Teachers <u>who get to know their students</u> are the (better (best)) mentors.
12. __P__ The cat <u>with the fluffy tail</u> is ((softer) softest) than my cat.
13. __C__ Mando's (new) newer) bike, <u>which he got for his birthday</u>, was stolen.
14. __P__ The (bigger (biggest)) home <u>in the neighborhood</u> costs the most.
15. __P__ The people <u>at the beach</u> enjoyed the ((warm) warmer) summer day.

Voyages in English 8 • Pre-test ~ Chapter 1 • 3

● **Underline the demonstrative, interrogative, or indefinite adjective in each sentence. Write DEM (demonstrative), INT (interrogative), or IND (indefinite) on the line. Then circle the correct comparative or superlative adjective to complete each sentence.**

16. __DEM__ <u>Those</u> flowers have (less (fewer)) petals than the daisies.
17. __DEM__ <u>Students</u> were given ((less) fewest) time for <u>these</u> presentations.
18. __INT__ <u>Which</u> pizza has the (fewest (least)) pepper?
19. __IND__ <u>Many</u> sports require ((less) fewer) strength.
20. __IND__ <u>Some</u> people donated ((fewer) least) canned foods than others.

● **Draw lines to connect each simple, overused word to two more exact, descriptive words.**

Overused Words: said, walk, fun, bad, pretty

21. playful
22. terrible
23. stroll
24. remarked
25. lovely

(entertaining, cried, awful, gorgeous, amble)

● **Put the following events in the order they would appear on a time line. Number them 1–6.**

26. __4__ stem grows from shoot
27. __2__ shoot emerges from seed casing
28. __6__ flower blooms
29. __3__ shoot breaks ground
30. __5__ leaves grow from stem
31. __1__ seed is planted

● **Write S (simple), CD (compound), or CX (complex) to identify the type of each sentence.**

32. __S__ Britney's new hat has pink and purple flowers.
33. __CX__ Rebecca, who is also known as Becky, came to visit last week.
34. __S__ Please let me know what kind of dessert to bring.
35. __CD__ Mia likes chocolate ice cream, but Siena likes strawberry.
36. __CD__ Cats enjoy balls of yarn, but dogs prefer tennis balls.
37. __CX__ Though we were late for the meeting, we were still able to vote.

4 • Chapter 1 ~ Pre-test Voyages in English 8

CHAPTER 1 Post-test

- **Write the possessive form of the first noun or nouns in parentheses and the plural form of the second noun in parentheses. Then underline count nouns once and noncount nouns twice.**

1. (Tim and Jill) **Tim's and Jill's** papers discuss animal (baby) **babies**.
2. (Jess) **Jess's** mother cooked (broccoli) **broccoli** for the picnic.
3. The (children) **children's** (clothes) **clothes** were wet from the rain.
4. The rules of the math (teacher) **teacher's** game gave students four (try) **tries** to solve the puzzle.

- **Identify the use of the underlined nouns in each sentence. Write S (subject), SC (subject complement), DO (direct object), ID (indirect object), or OC (object complement) on the lines.**

5. **OC** We named the pig Giggles after its personality.
6. **S, OC** The cheer squad chose Keisha captain for the semester.
7. **S, DO** Devon gave his jacket to the shivering child.
8. **S, SC** My sister is a very talented piano player.

- **Underline the adjective phrase or clause in each sentence. Identify it by writing P (phrase) or C (clause) on the line. Then circle the correct comparative or superlative adjective to complete each sentence.**

9. **P** The boy with the curly hair is the (smarter (smartest)) student of all.
10. **P** My truck in the garage is (fastest (faster)) than yours.
11. **P** Their (most amazing (more amazing)) stunt in the show came last.
12. **C** The ((spiciest) more spicy) food I've ever had is at Bill's BBQ.
13. **P** That shop is the (more expensive (most expensive)) store in New York.

- **Underline the demonstrative, interrogative, or indefinite adjective in each sentence. Write DEM, INT, or IND. Then circle the correct comparative or superlative adjective to complete each sentence.**

14. **DEM** That clerk has ((less) fewer) patience with customers.
15. **INT** Which student has read the ((fewest) least) books?
16. **DEM** Are there (fewest (fewer) cookies or brownies for those children?
17. **IND** Most students sitting in the back pay ((less) least) attention than those in the front.

- **Draw lines to connect each simple, overused word to two more exact, descriptive words.**

18. despise — loathe
19. intelligent — smart, brilliant
20. streak — race
21. polite — pleasant, nice
22. cherish — love, adore

Overused Words: run, love, smart, hate, nice

- **Put the following events in the order they would appear on a time line. Number them 2–6. The first one is done for you.**

23. **1** butterfly lays an egg
24. **4** caterpillar spins a chrysalis around itself
25. **5** caterpillar changes within chrysalis
26. **6** butterfly emerges from chrysalis
27. **3** caterpillar eats and matures
28. **2** egg becomes caterpillar

- **Write S (simple), CD (compound), or CX (complex) to identify the type of each sentence.**

29. **CD** Amanda used watercolors, but Jackson used oils.
30. **S** My family spent last summer in South America.
31. **CX** Dr. Wright, who is our veterinarian, owns two dogs and three snakes.
32. **S** Alicia grew lemons, apples, and oranges in her orchards.

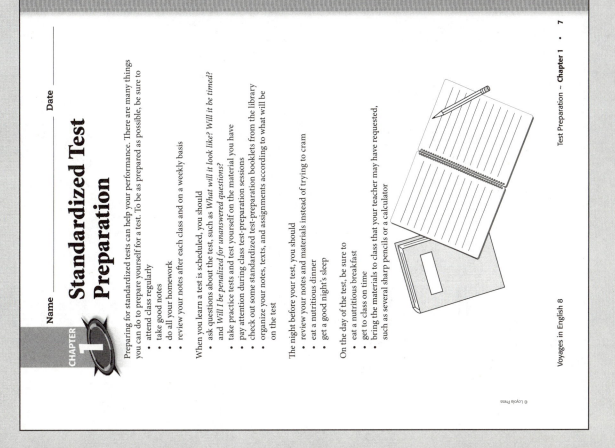

Name _____ Date _____

CHAPTER 1 — Standardized Test Preparation

Preparing for standardized tests can help your performance. There are many things you can do to prepare yourself for a test. To be as prepared as possible, be sure to
- attend class regularly
- take good notes
- do all your homework
- review your notes after each class and on a weekly basis

When you learn a test is scheduled, you should
- ask questions about the test, such as *What will it look like? Will it be timed?* and *Will I be penalized for unanswered questions?*
- take practice tests and test yourself on the material you have
- pay attention during class test-preparation sessions
- check out some standardized test-preparation booklets from the library
- organize your notes, texts, and assignments according to what will be on the test

The night before your test, you should
- review your notes and materials instead of trying to cram
- eat a nutritious dinner
- get a good night's sleep

On the day of the test, be sure to
- eat a nutritious breakfast
- get to class on time
- bring the materials to class that your teacher may have requested, such as several sharp pencils or a calculator

---

- **Write a word for each clue. Add each clue to the crossword puzzle.**

Across
3. Come to class with requested materials, such as sharpened _____.
5. Check out standardized test-preparation booklets from the _____.
7. Get a good night's _____ before the test.

Down
1. Always do all your _____.
2. Before the test, eat a _____ breakfast.
4. Do not _____ on the night before the test.
6. Review your notes on a _____ basis.

Answers:
Across: 3. PENCILS 5. LIBRARY 7. SLEEP
Down: 1. HOMEWORK 2. NUTRITIOUS 4. CRAM 6. WEEKLY

Name _____ Date _____

CHAPTER 1 Personal Narrative Scoring Rubric

- **In Chapter 1 you have written personal narratives. Read the personal narrative that you wrote for the prompt on page 9. Complete the following assessment.**

Personal Narrative	Yes	No
Ideas		
Does my piece show an apparent theme or purpose?		
Did I express the experience's importance?		
Organization		
Have I provided an engaging lead?		
Did I use a graphic organizer to plan?		
Did I use chronological order?		
Did I give a sense of resolution in the conclusion?		
Voice		
Does my piece show my personality?		
Have I provided a sense of authenticity?		
Have I used an appropriate tone?		
Word Choice		
Did I use exact words?		
Have I used natural language?		
Sentence Fluency		
Have I used a variety of sentence types?		
Have I used a variety of sentence lengths?		
Did I use transition words?		
Conventions		
Did I check for correct grammar and usage?		
Did I check for correct spelling?		
Did I check for correct punctuation?		

10 • Chapter 1 ~ Scoring Rubric   Voyages in English 8

Name _____ Date _____

CHAPTER 1 Personal Narrative Writing Prompt

Test items are often in the form of a prompt, a short paragraph that tells you what to write. Follow these suggestions when writing for a prompt.

1. Carefully read the prompt.
2. Circle the key words that signal the genre, in this case, a personal narrative, and key words that signal audience or purpose.
3. Plan your writing. You might use a word web, a time line, notes, or a short outline.
4. Write a draft based on your plan.
5. Read and revise your draft.
6. Proofread and copyedit your draft.

- **Write for the following prompt. Plan your writing on this page. Write your personal narrative on a separate sheet of paper.**

Prompt: Think about your first day of school. What do you want your parents to know about that experience? Share your memories of that day. Be sure to include what you saw and heard as well as how you felt.

Voyages in English 8   Writing Prompt ~ Chapter 1 • 9

CHAPTER 2 Pre-test

Name _____ Date _____

- **Underline the pronoun in each sentence. Circle S if it is a subject pronoun and O if it is an object pronoun. Then write the person and number of the pronoun.**

			Person	Number
1.	(S) O	Jane and I went to the mall yesterday.	first person	singular
2.	(S) O	We tried to visit Grandma yesterday.	first person	plural
3.	S (O)	Wendy used birthday money to buy them.	third person	plural
4.	S (O)	Afterward, Bill treated her to lunch.	third person	singular

- **Underline the intensive or reflexive pronoun in each sentence. Identify it by writing *intensive* or *reflexive*. Then circle the correct pronoun after *than* or *as*.**

5. The students themselves were quicker than (we) us). __intensive__
6. Brandon must prepare himself to speak as loud as (she) her). __reflexive__
7. Tara herself is better at spelling than (I) me). __intensive__
8. I enjoyed myself at the concert more than (he) him). __reflexive__

- **Circle the correct interrogative and demonstrative pronouns to complete each sentence. Then write the pronoun that agrees with the underlined antecedent.**

9. (Which) What) of the orchards produced (this (those)? We planted __them__ more than 10 years ago.
10. In studying the mountains, (what) which) did you find out about (that (those)? __They__ are majestic.
11. (Whose) Who) is the backpack that looks like (this) these)? __It__ must belong to Chelsea.
12. When you saw the butterflies at the nature center, did you see (these) this)? (Which) What) of __them__ do you think is the most beautiful?

Pre-test ~ Chapter 2 • 11

- **Underline each indefinite pronoun. Then circle the verb that agrees with it.**

13. Both (were) was) on the discussion panel.
14. Everyone (vote (votes)) on Election Day.
15. No one (go (goes)) to the baseball games any longer.
16. Someone (drive (drives)) my mom to the library every week.

- **Revise each sentence, trimming it so every word counts.**

17. To create a personal collage, first gather photos, drawings, and favorite words and phrases that you can glue to a piece of poster board to make the collage.
    Possible Answer: To create a personal collage, first gather photos, drawings, and favorite words and phrases.
18. Use scissors to cut out each piece and use glue to attach each piece to your poster board.
    Possible Answer: Cut out each piece and glue it to your poster board.
19. Finally, review your finished collage that you made, and think about a good title, and then write the title at the top.
    Possible Answer: Finally, review your finished collage and write a title at the top.

- **Draw a line to the meaning of the underlined root in each word.**

20. spectator — end
21. finale — carry
22. vocation — look
23. transport — call

(lines drawn: spectator→look, finale→end, vocation→call, transport→carry)

- **Read the following dictionary page guide words. If the words listed below would appear on this page, write *on*. If the words would appear before this page, write *before*. If the words would appear after this page, write *after*.**

CORONATION — COUNTER

24. counselor __on__   26. cornflakes __before__
25. course __after__   27. counterfeit __after__

12 • Chapter 2 ~ Pre-test

CHAPTER 2 Post-test

Name _____ Date _____

- **Underline the pronoun in each sentence. Circle S if it is a subject pronoun and O if it is an object pronoun. Then write the person and number of the pronoun.**

			Person	Number
1.	S (O)	Hannah carried <u>her</u> to bed.	third person	singular
2.	(S) O	<u>I</u> love the new television.	first person	singular
3.	S (O)	Carl is hoping to meet <u>them</u>.	third person	plural
4.	(S) O	<u>You</u> alone know how to help Mary.	second person	singular

- **Underline the intensive or reflexive pronoun in each sentence. Identify it by writing *intensive* or *reflexive*. Then circle the correct pronoun after *than* or *as*.**

5. Kaitlyn pushed <u>herself</u> to study as hard as (I) me). __reflexive__
6. Terrance and Katie <u>themselves</u> will lead the group as confidently as (us (we)). __intensive__
7. I told <u>myself</u> to stop worrying; I was as talented as (her (she)). __reflexive__
8. We <u>ourselves</u> should be skiing more skillfully than (they) them). __intensive__

- **Circle the correct interrogative and demonstrative pronouns to complete each sentence. Then write the pronoun that agrees with the underlined antecedent.**

9. (Who) Whom) bought (these (this))—the silver <u>bike</u>? __it__ looks new.
10. (What) Which) do you know about <u>Tom</u>? I think __he__ is an interesting person.
11. (Which) What) of (these) this) are your favorite <u>cookies</u>? __They__ are all delicious!
12. (Who (Whom)) <u>will you</u> ask to the dance? I think __you__ should ask Michael.

- **Underline each indefinite pronoun. Then circle the verb that agrees with it.**

13. Does <u>anyone</u> (want) wants) more dessert?
14. <u>Somebody</u> (writes) write) poetry that could be published.
15. <u>Several</u> (agree) agrees) to go to the movies on Friday.
16. <u>Everybody</u> (want (wants)) to take the puppy home tonight.

- **Revise each sentence, trimming it so every word counts.**

17. Cut and slice the vegetables into pieces shaped like cubes using a sharp knife.
    Sample answer: Use a sharp knife to cut the vegetables into cubes.
18. You may want to use a fork to pierce and stick the potatoes to make sure they are ready and finished boiling.
    _____

- **Draw a line to the meaning of the underlined root in each word.**

19. <u>derm</u>atology — skin
20. manu<u>script</u> — life
21. <u>audio</u> — see/watch
22. <u>micro</u>scope — hear
23. <u>bio</u>sphere — write

- **Read the following dictionary page guide words. If the words listed below would appear on this page, write *on*. If the words would appear before this page, write *before*. If the words would appear after this page, write *after*.**

FLEXIBILITY — FLOORING

24. flee __before__   26. flexible __on__
25. floppy __after__   27. float __on__

CHAPTER 2
Multiple-Choice Tips/ Using a Separate Answer Sheet

Name _____ Date _____

Multiple-choice items are commonly used for standardized tests. These items are written so that there is only one correct, or best, answer for each question. Each item lists several possible answers from which to choose. Some possible answers may seem to be "almost correct," so you must be careful when choosing the best answer.

To perform your best on multiple-choice tests, follow these tips:
- Before the test, check with your teacher to see if it is best to always mark an answer, even if you are not sure of which one is correct. Ask your teacher if you are graded only on the items you actually answer.
- Read all the directions before you begin the test.
- Read each question carefully.
- Read all answer choices before marking any answer.
- If you find a choice that states *all of the above*, consider only it if you are sure that two or more answers are correct.
- If you find a choice that states *none of the above*, consider only it if you are sure that two or more answers are incorrect.
- First, eliminate any answers that you know are incorrect. Then take your time to logically think about the remaining choices. Go back and reread the question if you need to.
- Watch out for choices that use words such as *never*, *always*, or *only*. These extreme words often signal an incorrect choice.
- If you are unsure of an answer, place a mark next to that item number on your answer sheet and move on to the next question. Come back to that question if there is time after finishing the rest of the test. Make an educated guess if your teacher recommended marking all the answers.

For standardized tests, you are often given a separate answer sheet on which to record your answers. When using separate answer sheets, do the following:
- Use only a #2 pencil to mark your answers. Do not use a pen or marker.
- Completely fill in each answer bubble.
- Do not cross out any mistakes. Erase them carefully.
- Do not fold or crease the answer sheet.
- From time to time, quickly review your answer sheet to be sure that you are on the correct number and that you didn't skip a row or section.
- Write only on your answer sheet. Do not write in your test booklet.

● **Answer the following multiple-choice questions, using the separate answer space below.**

1. When beginning a multiple-choice test, you should
   A. always start with the last question and work your way toward the front of the test.
   B. read the directions carefully.
   C. always mark the last answer as your choice.

2. *Always*, *never*, and *only* are words that often signal
   D. a correct choice.
   E. an incorrect choice.
   F. neither of the above.

3. One good question to ask your teacher before a multiple-choice test is,
   G. "Should I leave an item blank if I don't know the answer?"
   H. "When can we leave for lunch?"
   J. "May we use a dictionary?"

4. When taking the test,
   A. do not linger too long on any one question.
   B. use a #2 pencil.
   C. both of the above.

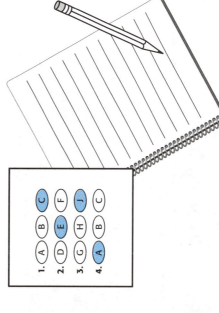

1. Ⓐ Ⓑ **C**
2. Ⓓ **E** Ⓕ
3. **G** Ⓗ **J**
4. **A** Ⓑ Ⓒ

Name _____ Date _____

CHAPTER 2
How-to Article Writing Prompt

Test items are often in the form of a prompt, a short paragraph that tells you what to write. Follow these suggestions when writing for a prompt.

1. Carefully read the prompt.
2. Circle the key words that signal the genre, in this case, a how-to article, and key words that signal audience or purpose.
3. Plan your writing. You might use a word web, a time line, notes, or a short outline.
4. Write a draft based on your plan.
5. Read and revise your draft.
6. Proofread and copyedit your draft.

• **Write for the following prompt. Plan your writing on this page. Write your how-to article on a separate sheet of paper.**

Prompt: Next summer your family is planning a two-week car trip through your state. Your parents have asked you to help plan the itinerary. What is the first thing you should do? What would be next? Write a how-to article for your family to help plan the best trip ever.

Writing Prompt ~ Chapter 2 • 17

Name _____ Date _____

CHAPTER 2
How-to Article Scoring Rubric

• **In Chapter 2 you have written how-to articles. Read the how-to article that you wrote for the prompt on page 17. Complete the following assessment.**

How-to Article	Yes	No
Ideas		
Have I given a clear purpose for the topic?		
Did I provide information that is detailed and complete?		
Organization		
Have I clearly identified in the introduction what the article will teach?		
Did I present the steps in the order they will be completed?		
Have I summarized what was taught?		
Voice		
Have I used an appropriate tone?		
Did I use imperative sentences to state my directions?		
Word Choice		
Did I use transition words?		
Have I used language specific to the topic?		
Sentence Fluency		
Have I used clear, concise sentences?		
Does my piece transition logically from step to step?		
Have I avoided run-on and rambling sentences?		
Conventions		
Did I check for correct grammar and usage?		
Did I check for correct spelling?		
Did I check for correct punctuation?		

18 • Chapter 2 ~ Scoring Rubric

Name _____ Date _____

CHAPTER 3 Pre-test

- **Underline the verb or verb phrase in each sentence. Write *present tense, past tense, present participle,* or *past participle* to identify the principal part of each verb. Then write *active* or *passive* to identify the voice of each verb.**

1. The dog grows tired of the game. — **present tense** — **active**
2. A lollipop was given to Manny. — **past participle** — **passive**
3. I am taking the book with me to class. — **present participle** — **active**
4. The reports were written by the students. — **past participle** — **passive**

- **Underline the verb or verb phrase in each sentence. Write *transitive* or *intransitive* to identify each verb.**

5. The guest speaker will provide answers to all of our questions. — **transitive**
6. A chilly wind blew through the trees. — **intransitive**
7. Several customers are waiting at the checkout line. — **intransitive**
8. Leslie donates money to several charitable organizations. — **transitive**

- **Circle the verb that correctly completes each sentence.**

9. Kris will (**bring**/take) her paints here.
10. The sleepy cat is (laying/**lying**) in the sun.
11. Did you (**set**/sit) the plant on the windowsill?
12. David (**lays**/lies) tile for a living.

- **Identify the mood the verb expresses by writing *indicative, imperative,* or *subjunctive.***

13. Those boys did play a good game of baseball. — **indicative**
14. I wish I had handled the situation differently. — **subjunctive**
15. Please clean your room today. — **imperative**
16. Shane will be studying for his final exam. — **indicative**

- **Circle the verb in parentheses that correctly completes each sentence. Then underline any auxiliary verbs.**

17. Brandon and Lin can (**solve**/solves) math problems quickly.
18. Everyone should (**strive**/strives) to do his or her best.
19. Jenna's hair and eyes (is/**are**) her best features.
20. (**There is**/There are) plenty of time to make dinner.

- **Draw a line to match the adjective or adverb clause that best completes each sentence. Then circle the noun or verb each clause modifies.**

21. The (game) _____ — a. until I finish this phone call
22. My (sister), _____, won the award. — b. that we played
23. Please don't (leave) _____ — c. who is a talented dancer

(21→b, 22→c, 23→a)

- **Circle the correct form of the compound word in parentheses to complete each sentence. Then write the clipped (shortened) form of each underlined word on the line.**

24. Jake left his (key board/**keyboard**) in the taxicab. — **taxi or cab**
25. Mia's (**father-in-law**/father in law) is a war veteran. — **vet**
26. She is a huge fanatic of (basket ball/**basketball**). — **fan**

- **Look at the completed check. Then answer the questions.**

```
Jerome Brooks                                  205
4555 Oak Drive
My Town, NY 11223                    20____  1-6/210

PAY TO THE
ORDER OF  All-Pro Sports Shop      $ 44.75
          Forty-four and 75/100            Dollars

NATIONAL BANK
My Town, NY 11223                  Jerome Brooks
For tennis racquet

⑆222333344⑆ 5556789900
```

27. What did Jerome buy? — **tennis racquet**
28. How much did it cost? — **$44.75**
29. What part of the check did Jerome forget to fill in? — **date**
30. To what store did Jerome write his check? — **All-Pro Sports Shop**

Name _____ Date _____

CHAPTER 3 Post-test

- Underline the verb or verb phrase in each sentence. Write *present tense, past tense, present participle,* or *past participle* to identify the principal part of each verb. Then write *active* or *passive* to identify the voice of each verb.

1. My sister teaches an advanced class. — **present tense** — **active**
2. The championship was won by our team. — **past participle** — **passive**
3. We are changing our clothes at the house. — **present participle** — **active**
4. Several packages were mailed by Marie. — **past participle** — **passive**

- Underline the verb or verb phrase in each sentence. Write *transitive* or *intransitive* to identify each verb.

5. The birds are singing in the tree outside my window. — **intransitive**
6. Tom and Teri work at the food pantry every Monday night. — **intransitive**
7. Sarah will place the boxes in the garage. — **transitive**
8. Our music teacher gives lessons after school. — **transitive**

- Circle the verb that correctly completes each sentence.

9. Please (**sit**) set) on the couch during the meeting.
10. Did you remember to (rise (**raise**)) the blinds this morning?
11. Ana (**borrowed**) lent) the racing bike from me.
12. The children always (**rise**) raise) early on Saturday mornings.

- Identify the mood the verb expresses by writing *indicative, imperative,* or *subjunctive*.

13. I do order many books and CDs online. — **indicative**
14. Bring your bathing suit along with you. — **imperative**
15. Mia's dog will have followed us home by then. — **indicative**
16. If Ben had eaten lunch, he might feel better. — **subjunctive**

Post-test ~ Chapter 3 • 21

- Circle the verb in parentheses that correctly completes each sentence. Then underline any auxiliary verbs.

17. Many of the participants may (leave (**leaves**)) before lunch.
18. Hiking tips and safety (is (**are**)) the subjects of the manual.
19. Neena and Manuel could (**try**) tries) harder to be on time.
20. Leah's dress and shoes (is (**are**)) covered with mud.

- Draw a line to the adjective or adverb clause that best completes each sentence. Then circle the noun or verb each clause modifies.

21. The (student) _____ — a. because I was busy writing notes
22. Let's (clean) the kitchen _____ — b. before we leave
23. I didn't (listen) _____ — c. who lost this backpack

(21→c, 22→b, 23→a)

- Circle the correct form of the compound word in parentheses to complete each sentence. Then write the clipped (shortened) form of each underlined word on the line.

24. My (**great-grandmother**) great-grandmother) was a veterinarian. — **vet**
25. We watched a moving picture at the ((**drive-in**) drive in). — **movie**
26. The (vice-president (**vice president**)) is on that airplane. — **plane**

- Look at the completed check. Then answer the questions.

```
Miranda Lake                                      712
9876 Prairie Circle
Any Town, NC 12312            May 15  20 05    3-7/909

PAY TO THE
ORDER OF  All About You Salon & Spa   $ 120.00
One hundred twenty-four and 00/100          Dollars

NATIONAL BANK
Any Town, NC 12312                    Miranda Lake

For facial and manicure
 333444455    67777888999
```

27. When did Miranda write this check? — **May 15, 2005**
28. What did she pay for? — **facial and manicure**
29. Why might Miranda's bank have trouble processing her check? — **the amount she wrote in numerals does not match the amount she wrote in words**

22 • Chapter 3 ~ Post-test

CHAPTER 3
Analyze Text: Nonfiction Elements

Name _____ Date _____

A test item might measure your ability to analyze nonfiction text.

The test item might look like this:

Read the passage. Answer the questions.

> The American Revolution began as a dispute over a fundamental power of a government, taxation. The British government had accrued enormous debt as a result of its war with France. It also had to pay to maintain a standing army in the thirteen colonies to guard against French interference. As a result, once the French and Indian War was brought to a close in 1763, the British subjected the colonies to trade restrictions and a series of taxes that benefited England. The British Parliament thought that this was fair because it had paid for the protection of the colonies. The colonists, however, took a different view. They felt that they were being taxed without having a voice in the matter. The phrase "no taxation without representation" became a common rallying cry from colonists. A series of clashes between colonists and the British government brought about open, armed rebellion by the colonists.

1. What power of government inspired the American Revolution?
   A. the army   C. taxation
   B. exploration   D. colonization

2. According to the passage, why did the British think their taxes were fair?
   A. The taxes paid for the colonists' protection.
   B. The colonists were lazy.
   C. Britain couldn't afford tea.
   D. Other colonies paid more taxes.

Read the passage carefully. Then read question 1 and all of the answer choices. You should choose the best answer for the question. You would choose C because taxation was the government power that inspired the American Revolution.

Read question 2 and all of the answer choices. You would choose A because the British felt the colonists should pay for their own protection.

Voyages in English 8 • Test Preparation ~ Chapter 3 • 23

• Read the passage. Answer the questions.

People have long sought to find ways to preserve food, but it wasn't until the late 18th and early 19th centuries that canning was invented. Napoleon needed a method to preserve food so that his armies could feed themselves on long campaigns. He offered a prize of 12,000 francs to the person who could find a way to reliably preserve food. A French candy maker named Nicholas Appert won the prize by devising a method of preserving food in glass jars. He experimented with various methods until he discovered that steam heating food in jars killed microorganisms that caused food to spoil. Shortly thereafter an Englishman named Charles Durand began sealing food in tin containers. The practice spread to America and was widely imitated and refined so that canning factories could produce large quantities of canned foods within hours.

1. Why did Napoleon want preserved foods?
   A to cut costs for his navy
   B to give citizens food that tasted better
   C to feed his army on long campaigns
   D to feed the growing American market

1.  (C selected)

2. The winner of Napoleon's prize was
   F Benjamin Franklin
   G Charles Durand
   H Louis Pasteur
   J Nicholas Appert

2.  (J selected)

3. Steam heating preserved foods by
   K drying food out
   L killing microorganisms in food
   M removing bad odors
   N washing away dirt

3. (L selected)

24 • Chapter 3 ~ Test Preparation

Name _____ Date _____

CHAPTER 3

Business Letter
Writing Prompt

Test items are often in the form of a prompt, a short paragraph that tells you what to write. Follow these suggestions when writing for a prompt.

1. Carefully read the prompt.
2. Circle the key words that signal the genre, in this case, a business letter, and key words that signal audience or purpose.
3. Plan your writing. You might use a word web, a time line, notes, or a short outline.
4. Write a draft based on your plan.
5. Read and revise your draft.
6. Proofread and copyedit your draft.

- **Write for the following prompt. Plan your writing on this page. Write your business letter on a separate sheet of paper.**

Prompt: Your basketball team needs a corporate sponsor. Write a letter to a local business leader asking his or her organization to sponsor your team. Explain why it needs support and how the company could benefit. Be sure to include all parts of a business letter.

Name _____ Date _____

CHAPTER 3

Business Letter
Scoring Rubric

- **In Chapter 3 you have written business letters. Read the business letter that you wrote for the prompt on page 25. Complete the following assessment.**

Business Letter	Yes	No
Ideas		
Did I clearly state the reason for writing the letter?		
Did I provide detailed information that is tailored to the recipient?		
Organization		
Have I used correct business letter format?		
Did I present the facts in logical order?		
Voice		
Have I used a strong voice?		
Have I used a persuasive voice?		
Have I used a respectful voice?		
Word Choice		
Does my piece reflect business letter etiquette?		
Have I used compound words correctly?		
Have I used a formal tone?		
Sentence Fluency		
Did I articulate the problem and solutions?		
Have I used adjective and adverb clauses?		
Does my piece flow from one sentence to the next?		
Conventions		
Did I check for correct grammar and usage?		
Did I check for correct spelling?		
Did I check for correct punctuation?		

Name _____ Date _____

CHAPTER 4 Pre-test

- **Underline the participial phrase in each sentence. Then circle the participle.**
  1. Jason, (having driven) the car across country, was extremely tired.
  2. Miranda watched the tiny baby (sleeping) in the crib.
  3. (Admired) by all in the class, our guest speaker concluded his speech.
  4. (Left) in the rain, my backpack became soaking wet.
  5. The sound of children (laughing) loudly filled the theater.
  6. While (sitting) in his bed, my dog became startled and growled.

- **Underline the gerund phrase in each sentence. Then identify it by writing S (subject), SC (subject complement), DO (direct object), OP (object of a preposition), or A (appositive).**
  7. My dream, climbing Half Dome in Yosemite, will finally be realized. __A__
  8. Brianna started her career by working her way up from the bottom. __OP__
  9. Most people love opening presents on their birthday. __DO__
  10. A good way to make friends is smiling at people you don't know. __SC__
  11. Skiing in fresh, powdery snow is a great way to learn the sport. __S__

- **Underline the infinitive phrase in each sentence. Then identify it by writing S (subject), SC (subject complement), O (object), or A (appositive).**
  12. It was her wish to save enough money for softball camp. __A__
  13. I started to write my final paper well before the due date. __O__
  14. Our favorite activity is to hike to the mountaintop for a picnic. __SC__
  15. To hold open doors for people is showing good manners. __S__

- **Underline the infinitive or infinitive phrase in each sentence. Then identify it by writing N (noun), ADJ (adjective), or ADV (adverb).**
  16. Therese wanted to sculpt a replica of Michelangelo's David. __N__
  17. Traveling across the country was a great way to learn more about other states. __ADJ__
  18. Helene would rather write the report than read it aloud. __N__
  19. Wolf was too hungry to stop eating. __ADV__

- **Place the following information in the Venn diagram.**

  four legs   reptile   eats mice   slithers   tail
  fangs   walks   no legs   eats insects   scales
  cold-blooded

  Topic: Snake / Topic: Lizard

  Snake only: eats mice, fangs, slithers, no legs
  Both: scales, cold-blooded, reptile
  Lizard only: eats insects, four legs, tail, walks

- **Write simile, metaphor, personification, or hyperbole to identify the figure of speech used in each sentence.**
  20. That spicy pizza set my hair on fire! __hyperbole__
  21. The baby's hair felt as soft as silk. __simile__
  22. The trees whispered in the gentle breeze. __personification__
  23. Her laugh tinkles like tiny bells ringing. __simile__
  24. That cheetah is a silent watchman, waiting for its prey. __metaphor__
  25. I nearly died laughing. __hyperbole__

- **Look up the word *superficial* in a thesaurus. Write the page number on which you found the word, and write at least three possible synonyms for it. Use one of the synonyms you found in a sentence.**

  page number: __Answers will vary.__
  three synonyms: __Answers will vary.__
  sentence with one synonym: __Answers will vary.__

Name _____ Date _____

CHAPTER 4 Post-test

- **Underline the participial phrase in each sentence. Then circle the participle.**
  1. As the cat watched, the rapidly (scurrying) mouse ran for the shadows.
  2. The carrot cake (baked) by my mother won a blue ribbon at the state fair.
  3. Many of these animals, (beloved) by their former owners, will find good homes.
  4. (Having scored) the highest grade, Michael felt proud of himself.
  5. Our cat, (moving) in fits and starts, evidently needed a tune-up.

- **Underline the gerund or the gerund phrase in each sentence. Then identify it by writing S (subject), SC (subject complement), DO (direct object), OP (object of a preposition), or A (appositive).**
  6. Eating fresh, organic foods is a good strategy for good health. _____ S
  7. Jessica has the personality for making people feel comfortable. _____ OP
  8. One of my favorite weekend comforts is sleeping late. _____ SC
  9. My report topic, finding new ways to conserve energy, was approved. _____ A
  10. Mom tried staying calm as we baked cookies in her clean kitchen. _____ DO

- **Underline the infinitive phrase in each sentence. Then identify it by writing S (subject), SC (subject complement), O (object), or A (appositive).**
  11. To attend a four-year university is the goal of many students. _____ S
  12. My best friend likes to tutor the younger students at school. _____ O
  13. Our job, to paint the lifeguard towers, took all summer long. _____ A
  14. Taylor's ambition is to create the most advanced science project. _____ SC

- **Underline the infinitive or infinitive phrase in each sentence. Then identify it by writing N (noun), ADJ (adjective), ADV (adverb), H (hidden), or S (split).**
  15. Lauren offered to help the teacher put away the supplies. — N
  16. It was the best idea to have come from the committee. — ADJ
  17. Please try to report specifically on each event. — N
  18. I visited my grandparents to talk with them about our family history. — ADV
  19. Carlos will not dare pass on this exceptional opportunity. — N

Post-test ~ Chapter 4 • 29

- **Place the following information in the Venn diagram.**

  Civil War   born in February   famous president   Virginia
  1st president   Illinois   Revolutionary War   16th president

  Topic: Abraham Lincoln   Topic: George Washington

  Left circle: Civil War, Illinois, 16th president
  Overlap: famous president, born in February
  Right circle: Revolutionary War, Virginia, 1st president

- **Write simile, metaphor, personification, or hyperbole to identify the figure of speech used in each sentence.**
  20. Hanna's prom dress is a pink cloud billowing around her. _____ metaphor
  21. Nora Chatham's new novel is a window into her soul. _____ metaphor
  22. Rain danced playfully over the rooftops of the small town. _____ personification
  23. Quiet as a whisper, the cat crept down the staircase. _____ simile
  24. I tried a thousand times to memorize the poem. _____ hyperbole
  25. The cloud scattered rain throughout the city. _____ personification
  26. The old man's face was as wrinkled as an elephant's hide. _____ simile

- **Look up the word demonstrate in a thesaurus. Write the page number on which you found the word, and write at least three possible synonyms for it. Use one of the synonyms you found in a sentence.**

  page number: _____ Answers will vary.
  three synonyms: _____ Answers will vary.
  sentence with one synonym: _____ Answers will vary.

30 • Chapter 4 ~ Post-test

Name _____ Date _____

CHAPTER 4
Writing Strategies: Using an Outline

An outline is a tool to organize your writing. An outline simplifies the writing process and keeps your thoughts unified. A test item that could measure your ability to create or use an outline might look like this.

You are writing a report on how to select a college. Your paper would include several paragraphs that would help a reader determine how to choose a college. Which of the following might be your choices for three main topics to outline?

A
 I. Why go to Notre Dame
 II. What makes college fun
 III. Must be no more than four hours from home

B
 I. Areas of study
 II. Geographical preferences
 III. Campus critiques

C
 I. Why go to college
 II. Pre-med studies
 III. Sports life at college

D
 I. Taking the ACT
 II. Scholarships
 III. Dorm life

As you read each answer choice, imagine that it is connected to the main idea of your outline. Ask yourself:
• Do these choices logically support the main idea of your outline?
• Do these choices cover a range of topics important in selecting a college?
• Is it the best choice of all?

You would then select the choices that best support an outline covering the important information needed to write your report. In the example, you would choose answer B because it
• supports the main idea, offering a range of information.
• helps develop the main idea of the outline.

• **Answer the questions by filling in the circle of the correct response.**

1. Which is the best title for an outline about the following paragraph?

> Illinois is home to more than 850 different species of plant life. Illinois is considered a prairie state because of its extensive grasslands. A prairie is considered a vegetative community dominated by many grasses and colorful flowers. Wild onions are also considered prairie plants. There are several different types of these. The Illinois state prairie grass is the big blue stem. The state flower is the blue violet.

A Illinois has many plants.
B State Flower: Blue Violet
C Roses that Grow in my Yard
D Illinois Prairie Plants

1. Ⓐ Ⓑ Ⓒ ●D

2. Identify the error in the outline below.

> Presidents of the United States 1950–1960
> I. Harry Truman
>   A. The Fair Deal
>   B. North Atlantic Treaty Alliance (NATO)
> II. Dwight Eisenhower
>   A. The Korean War
>   1. The Cold War.

F There is no middle initial listed for Harry Truman.
G "The Cold War" should be listed as B, not 1.
H Richard Nixon should be listed as Vice President under II.
J The title of the outline should be Presidents of the United States 1980–1990.

2. Ⓕ ●G Ⓗ Ⓙ

CHAPTER 4

Description
Writing Prompt

Name _____ Date _____

Test items are often in the form of a prompt, a short paragraph that tells you what to write. Follow these suggestions when writing for a prompt.

1. Carefully read the prompt.
2. Circle the key words that signal the genre, in this case, a description, and key words that signal audience or purpose.
3. Plan your writing. You might use a word web, a time line, notes, or a short outline.
4. Write a draft based on your plan.
5. Read and revise your draft.
6. Proofread and copyedit your draft.

• **Write for the following prompt. Plan your writing on this page. Write your description on a separate sheet of paper.**

Prompt: Think about the holidays you celebrate during the year. Choose two holidays and write a comparative description. Be sure to use sensory details. Include a good introduction, body, and conclusion.

CHAPTER 4

Description
Scoring Rubric

Name _____ Date _____

• **In Chapter 4 you have written descriptions. Read the description that you wrote for the prompt on page 33. Complete the following assessment.**

Description	Yes	No
Ideas		
Have I compared and contrasted two related subjects?		
Did I give equal weight to both subjects?		
Organization		
Did I name the two subjects in the introduction?		
Did I use logical sentence and paragraph order?		
Did I sum up the comparison in the conclusion?		
Voice		
Have I written appropriately for my audience?		
Will my piece grab and hold the reader's attention?		
Word Choice		
Have I used literary techniques such as analogies, point of view, and tone?		
Did I provide rich sensory details?		
Have I employed connecting words or phrases?		
Sentence Fluency		
Have I used a variety of sentence types, including those with noun clauses?		
Does my piece show natural transitions between sentences?		
Conventions		
Did I check for correct grammar and usage?		
Did I check for correct spelling?		
Did I check for correct punctuation and capitalization?		

CHAPTER 5 Pre-test

Name _____ Date _____

- **Circle the adverb in each sentence. Correct any adverb that is incorrect. Then identify each adverb by writing *interrogative, adverbial noun, comparative,* or *superlative.***

1. Compared with Arnie and Joe, Dan played (best) in the tournament. — **superlative**
2. (Where) did you put Grandpa's old journals? — **interrogative**
3. Kaitlyn always sleeps (longer) than her sister does. — **comparative**
4. Today we spent four (hours) hiking. — **adverbial noun**

- **Underline the adverb phrases and clauses in the following sentences.**

5. We climbed the mountain trail <u>until we were out of breath</u>.
6. When we got to the mountaintop, we ate a picnic lunch.
7. We reached our campsite <u>late in the afternoon</u>.
8. Our family sat <u>around the campfire</u> and told stories.

- **Circle the preposition that correctly completes the sentence.**

9. How did you choose (between) among) those two pairs of shoes?
10. In spite of his apology Jessie is still angry (at (with)) her best friend.
11. After Carl put his books (in (into)) his backpack, he rode away.
12. We differ (on) with) the kinds of flowers we want to plant in the backyard.

- **Underline the prepositional phrase in each sentence. Then identify how the prepositional phrase is used by writing *adjective, adverb,* or *noun*.**

13. During the Great Depression, work was scarce. — **adverb**
14. These flowers bloom only <u>at night</u>. — **adverb**
15. Darryl became a volunteer <u>in the Peace Corps</u>. — **adjective**
16. On the shaded patio is the best resting place. — **noun**
17. She was treated <u>like a member of the family</u>. — **adjective**

- **Write *.gov, .edu, .mil, .org, (state).us,* or *.com* to identify the domain code of the URL (address) you would look for to research each topic.**

18. How to write to your state representative — **(state).us**
19. Rain forest preservation organizations — **.org**
20. How to become a Marine — **.mil**
21. Local community college schedules — **.edu**
22. Visiting the White House — **.gov**
23. Locations of your favorite department store — **.com**

- **Rewrite each sentence with a noun clause. Use the word in parentheses to begin the noun clause. Remember, a noun clause can come at the beginning or end of a sentence.**

24. We would choose the restaurant for the wedding, and it was understood. (that)
    That we would choose the restaurant for the wedding was understood. OR It was understood that we would choose the restaurant for the wedding.
25. I wish to dance the lead in the recital, and it is my hope. (that)
    That I dance the lead in the recital is my hope. OR It is my hope that I dance the lead in the recital.
26. Our flight times got mixed up, and it is a mystery how it happened. (how)
    How our flight times got mixed up is a mystery. OR It is a mystery how our flight times got mixed up.
27. Tera didn't call to tell us she wasn't coming, and it bothered us. (why)
    Why Tera didn't call to tell us she wasn't coming bothered us. OR It bothered us that Tera didn't call to tell us she wasn't coming.

- **Write your best definition of each word based on the meaning of the prefix.**
  Possible answers

28. If *antisocial* means "not social," then *antifreeze* means ***not freezing**
29. If *redo* means "to do again," then *reappear* means ***to appear again**
30. If *overpriced* means "too much price," then *overactive* means ***too active**
31. If *biannual* means "twice a year," then *bimonthly* means ***twice a month**
32. If *postdate* means "to date after," then *postwar* means ***after war**
33. If *immobile* means "not mobile," then *immature* means ***not mature**

Name _____ Date _____

CHAPTER 5 Post-test

- **Circle the adverb in each sentence. Correct any adverb that is incorrect. Then identify each adverb by writing *interrogative*, *relative*, *adverbial noun*, *comparative*, or *superlative*.**

1. The performer greeted (most enthusiastically) was the clown. — **superlative**
2. Tyler measured six (cups) of rice into the big pot. — **adverbial noun**
3. Sheila asked, "(Why) weren't you at the meeting?" — **interrogative**
4. Casey was running (fastest) in the two-man race. — **comparative**

- **Underline the adverb phrases and clauses in the following sentences.**

5. The child dropped the ball and it rolled <u>under the bed</u>.
6. <u>When the presentation is over</u>, the speaker will answer questions.
7. Our tour begins early <u>in the morning</u>.
8. I will plant the tree <u>where there is room for it to grow</u>.

- **Circle the words that correctly complete the sentences.**

9. She could not decide (between / (among)) all the vacation packages to Rome.
10. ((Between laps) / Between every lap) we rested.
11. ((Besides) / Beside) my father, my brother likes working on cars in the garage.
12. I generally choose (between) / among) French toast and pancakes for breakfast.

- **Underline the prepositional phrase in each sentence. Then identify how the prepositional phrase is used by writing *adjective*, *adverb*, or *noun*.**

13. Justin is a private <u>in the U.S. Army</u>. — **adjective**
14. <u>After the flood</u>, relief workers helped the homeowners. — **adverb**
15. The kitten's favorite hiding place is <u>behind the curtains</u>. — **adverb**
16. The cheerleaders wore uniforms <u>in bright colors</u>. — **adjective**

Post-test ~ Chapter 5 • 37

- **Circle the word that correctly completes each sentence.**

17. My kitten was ((as) / so) playful as your puppy.
18. Cid's car doesn't go ((as) / so) fast as Serena's car.
19. That dress is ((as) / so) beautiful as this one.
20. The two applicants are ((equally) / equally as) qualified for the job.

- **Write *.gov*, *.edu*, *.mil*, *.org*, *(state).us*, or *.com* to identify the domain code of the URL (address) you would look for to research each topic.**

21. Where to send a donation to the World Wildlife Federation — **.org**
22. Library of Congress — **.gov**
23. Facts about your state flower, animal, and flag — **(state).us**
24. Stanford University swim team — **.edu**

- **Rewrite each sentence with a noun clause. Use the word in parentheses to begin the noun clause. Remember, a noun clause can come at the beginning or at the end of a sentence.**

25. Jonas told a tall tale: he had rescued 10 people from a burning building. (that)
    Jonas told a tall tale that he had rescued 10 people from a burning building.
26. There are 40 girls trying out for the softball team, and it is a fact. (that)
    It is a fact that 40 girls are trying out for the softball team. OR That 40 girls are trying out for the softball team is a fact.
27. The Pilgrims made it to the New World on the *Mayflower*, and it fascinates me. (how)
    How the Pilgrims made it to the New World on the Mayflower fascinates me. OR It fascinates me how the Pilgrims made it to the New World on the Mayflower.

- **Write your best definition of each word based on the meaning of the prefix.**
    Possible answers

28. If *pretreat* means "to treat before," then *prerecord* means ***to record before***.
29. If *international* means "among nations," then *intercollegiate* means ***among colleges***.
30. If *unable* means "not able," then *uncertain* means ***not certain***.
31. If *miscount* means "to count badly," then *mismanage* means ***to manage badly***.

38 • Chapter 5 ~ Post-test

Name _____ Date _____

CHAPTER 5
Sentence Structure: Misplaced Modifiers

A modifier is a word or group of words that modifies or describes something in a sentence. Some test items might measure your ability to understand where a modifier belongs in a sentence so that it describes the right word or the right group of words.

The test item might look like this:

The sentence in the box contains a misplaced modifier. Choose the best version of the sentence from the choices below.

> He published an article about the American Revolution in 1999.

A He, in 1999, published an article about the American Revolution.
B He published an article in 1999 about the American Revolution.
C He published an article about 1999 in the American Revolution.
D In 1999 he published an article about the American Revolution.

As you read each answer choice imagine what word the author is trying to further describe. Ask yourself:
  Which modifier is misplaced?
  Where is the best place for the modifier so it clearly indicates the intended meaning?

In the example, *in 1999* should modify the word *published*. You would then choose the placement that best modifies the word. In the example, you would choose answer B because

• *in 1999* is in the best position to be clearly understood.

Voyages in English 8   Test Preparation ~ Chapter 5 • 39

---

1. The sentence in the box contains a misplaced modifier. Choose the best version of the sentence from the choices below.

> Since the soccer match is next Monday, Macy almost practiced dribbling for an hour.

A Since the soccer match is next Monday, Macy practiced dribbling for almost an hour.
B Since the soccer match is almost next Monday, Macy practiced dribbling for an hour.
C Since the soccer match is next Monday almost, Macy practiced dribbling for an hour.
D Since the soccer match is next Monday, Macy practiced almost dribbling for an hour.

1. (**A**) B C D

2. Find the sentence that best places the modifier.

F Last night I tried to unsuccessfully ride a skateboard.
G Unsuccessfully, last night I tried to ride a skateboard.
H Last night I tried unsuccessfully to ride a skateboard.
J Last unsuccessfully night I tried to ride a skateboard.

2. F G (**H**) J

3. The sentence in the box contains a misplaced modifier. Choose the best version of the sentence from the choices below.

> The two-year-old reminds Jason of his cousin in the highchair.

K In the highchair the two-year-old reminds Jason of his cousin.
L The two-year-old reminds Jason in the highchair of his cousin.
M Jason is reminded of his two-year-old cousin in the highchair.
N The two-year-old in the highchair reminds Jason of his cousin.

3. K L M (**N**)

40 • Chapter 5 ~ Test Preparation   Voyages in English 8

Name _____ Date _____

CHAPTER 5
Expository Essay
Writing Prompt

Test items are often in the form of a prompt, a short paragraph that tells you what to write. Follow these suggestions when writing for a prompt.

1. Carefully read the prompt.
2. Circle the key words that signal the genre, in this case, an expository essay, and key words that signal audience or purpose.
3. Plan your writing. You might use a word web, a time line, notes, or a short outline.
4. Write a draft based on your plan.
5. Read and revise your draft.
6. Proofread and copyedit your draft.

- **Write for the following prompt. Plan your writing on this page. Write your expository essay on a separate sheet of paper.**

Prompt: Think of a favorite earth science topic, such as plate tectonics, the water cycle, a part of the solar system, or a weather-related topic. Write an expository essay that gives important facts about the topic. Be sure to identify your topic in the introduction.

Writing Prompt ~ **Chapter 5** • 41

Name _____ Date _____

CHAPTER 5
Expository Essay
Scoring Rubric

- **In Chapter 5 you have written expository essays. Read the essay that you wrote for the prompt on page 41. Complete the following assessment.**

Expository Essay

	Yes	No
Ideas		
Do I have a clear focus on one topic?		
Did I provide factual information supported by research or personal experience?		
Organization		
Did I include an interesting introduction with a topic sentence?		
Did I provide a logically ordered body of main ideas and details?		
Did I include a summarizing conclusion with insights?		
Voice		
Does the essay have a confident voice?		
Word Choice		
Did I use formal language?		
Sentence Fluency		
Did I use concise sentences?		
Did I provide information in varied ways?		
Did I use parallel sentence structure?		
Conventions		
Did I check for correct grammar?		
Did I check for correct spelling?		
Did I check for correct punctuation and capitalization?		

42 • **Chapter 5** ~ Scoring Rubric

CHAPTER 6 Pre-test

Name _____ Date _____

- **Underline each adjective phrase once and each adverb phrase twice. Write PREP (prepositional), PART (participial), or INF (infinitive) on the lines to identify each phrase according to type.**

1. These activities are part of a special sports program for children.   **PREP, PREP**
2. This special program was started in 1980.   **PREP**
3. The program, having won many awards, continues to grow.   **PART**
4. The program also provides opportunities to build children's self-esteem.   **INF**

- **Underline the adjective clauses once and the adverb clauses twice. Write R (restrictive) or NR (nonrestrictive) above each adjective clause.**

5. The elephants that did tricks made the audience laugh.   **R**
6. When Fluffy heard the thunder, she hid under the bed.
7. Summer, which is my favorite season, is only two months away.   **NR**
8. We tried to help so that Mom might get some rest.

- **Underline the noun clause in each sentence. Write S (subject), SC (subject complement), A (appositive), DO (direct object), or OP (object of preposition) to identify how each is used in the sentence.**

9. We learned about which of these foods are most healthful.   **OP**
10. The best advice was that good foods are rich in vitamins and protein.   **SC**
11. It is a medical myth that people should avoid fats altogether.   **A**
12. We decided that we would start eating more healthful foods.   **DO**
13. That we needed to exercise more frequently was also obvious.   **S**

- **Identify each kind of sentence by writing simple, compound, or complex.**

14. Before I could stop him, Rascal jumped out of the soapy tub.   **complex**
15. I chased him around and around the backyard.   **simple**
16. Rascal hated baths, but he needed one at least twice a month.   **compound**
17. When I finally caught him, Rascal was covered with mud.   **complex**
18. Apparently, I would have to start all over again!   **simple**

- **Identify the propaganda device used in each statement.**

| bandwagon | loaded words | testimonial | vague or sweeping generalities |

19. Everyone is laughing about this hilarious new movie!   **bandwagon**
20. Guaranteed lowest prices in the whole Northwest!   **vague or sweeping generalities**
21. Hollywood insider, Tommy Tux, won't use anything else.   **testimonial**
22. Some of us need those extra special minutes for phoning loved ones.   **loaded words**

- **Circle the transition word or phrase that correctly completes each sentence.**

23. Simon plays the piano; (therefore (**furthermore**)) he is a talented composer.
24. The rain poured down in buckets ((**until**) because) the whole yard was flooded.
25. Tia failed the final; (besides (**as a result**)) she had to repeat the class.
26. Manny decided to attend college ((**after**) unlike) he quit his job.

- **Add a suffix to each italicized word to create a new word that correctly completes the sentence. Write the new word on the line.**

27. I tiptoed *silent* past the sleeping baby's room.   **silently**
28. My best friend shows his *kind* in many ways.   **kindness**
29. My mother just completed her degree in child *develop*.   **development**
30. Please try to *familiar* yourself with your surroundings.   **familiarize**

CHAPTER 6 Post-test

Name _____ Date _____

- **Underline each adjective phrase once and each adverb phrase twice. Write PREP (prepositional), PART (participial), or INF (infinitive) on the lines to identify each phrase according to type.**

1. Those horses are a group of purebreds from Spain. — **PREP, PREP**
2. Many horses are trained to perform in international shows. — **INF, PREP**
3. Having owned many horses, I think the ones from Spain are the best. — **PART, PREP**
4. Horse shows occur across the entire country. — **PREP**

- **Underline each adjective clause once and each adverb clause twice. Write R (restrictive) or NR (nonrestrictive) above each adjective clause.**

5. Min, who is favored to win, will run the race tomorrow morning. — **NR**
6. The clothes that I bought are perfect for the trip. — **R**
7. When the lights went out, we lit candles so we could see.
8. I gave the speech because Jesse had a sore throat. — **R**

- **Underline the noun clause in each sentence. Write S (subject), SC (subject complement), A (appositive), DO (direct object), or OP (object of preposition) to identify how each is used in the sentence.**

9. Josh studied about what are the most harmful kinds of sharks. — **OP**
10. It is a fact that most sharks are harmless to people. — **A**
11. He realized that sharks have gotten a bad reputation for no reason. — **DO**
12. The truth is that sharks have existed for millions of years. — **SC**
13. That sharks are fascinating creatures was Josh's conclusion. — **S**

- **Identify each kind of sentence by writing simple, compound, or complex.**

14. Many people are fascinated by our ever-changing universe. — **simple**
15. The sun, which is the center of our universe, is actually a star. — **complex**
16. Mercury is the planet closest to the sun. — **simple**
17. Earth is the only planet known to have life, yet we need to keep exploring. — **compound**

- **Identify the propaganda device used in each statement.**

| bandwagon | loaded words | testimonial | vague or sweeping generalities |

18. Make Mom's day unforgettable with flowers from Norville's. — **loaded words**
19. Round up some Sizzle Sauce—the hottest sauce in the West! — **vague or sweeping generalities**
20. Everyone's reading *Hollywood Tales*—now it's your turn! — **bandwagon**
21. Supermodel Kristin Shane swears this lotion will take years off your face. — **testimonial**

- **Circle the transition word or phrase that correctly completes each sentence.**

22. I'm tired; (therefore) to begin with), I won't be joining you for golf.
23. Many volunteers helped at the bake sale; (while (in addition)) they donated money.
24. Ian felt sick to her stomach; (yet (consequently)) she went home from school.
25. The library is closed this weekend, (so) namely) we'll have to meet somewhere else.

- **Add a suffix to each italicized word to create a new word that correctly completes the sentence. Write the new word on the line.**

26. Adding more roses will surely make *beautiful* this garden. — **beautify**
27. Try not to *fright* the cat when you come in. — **frighten**
28. Marco is studying in Italy to be a *sculpt*. — **sculptor**
29. Don't be so *care* as to leave your car doors unlocked. — **careless**

CHAPTER 6
Editing Skills: Proofreading

Some test items might measure your ability to proofread or understand proofreader's marks.

The test item might look like this:

Proofread the paragraph below and select the answer that identifies the corrections to be made to the underlined words.

> California became a state on <u>september 9, 1850</u>. It was the 31st state <u>admits</u> to the Union. The <u>capitol of California</u> is Sacramento.

A September, admittance, capitol
B September, admitted, capital
C sept., admitted, capital
D September, admited, Capitol

As you read each answer choice, proofread to determine how to correct the underlined words. Ask yourself,
What does the whole sentence mean?
Why is each underlined word incorrect? Is it faulty grammar, capitalization, or punctuation?
What can I do to each underlined word to make it correct?

You would then choose the answer that corrects each underlined word. In the example, you would choose answer B. You would choose answer B because
- the first underlined word is a proper noun and should be capitalized.
- the second underlined word has the wrong verb tense and should be in the past tense.
- the third underlined word is spelled incorrectly and should end in -al.

---

1. Proofread the paragraph below and select the answer that identifies the corrections to be made to the underlined words.

   > Giani has <u>plan</u> to have his birthday party in <u>St Louis, missouri</u>.

   A planned, St., Missouri
   B planning, street, misouri
   C planed, st., Missouri
   D planned, st, misouri

   1. (A) ● B ○ C ○ D

2. Select the answer that identifies the correct meaning for a proofreading mark.

   F A ⊙ mark means add a new paragraph.
   G The ∧ mark means to insert or add something.
   H The / mark through a letter means to make it a capital letter.
   J "D" means to delete something.

   2. F ● G H J

3. Select the answer below that corrects the sentence in the box.

   > The Executive Branch of our government includes the office of the President
   > and other officials such as members of the Cabinet. ∧ Vice

   K The Executive Branch of our government includes the office of the Vice President and other officials such as members of the Cabinet.
   L The Executive Branch of our government includes the office of the vice President and other officials such as members of the Cabinet.
   M The Executive Branch of our government includes the office of the president and other officials such as members of the Cabinet.
   N The Executive Branch of our government includes the Vice President and other officials such as members of the cabinet.

   3. ● K L M N

Name _____ Date _____

CHAPTER 6
Persuasive Essay Scoring Rubric

- In Chapter 6 you wrote persuasive essays. Read the essay that you wrote for the prompt on page 49. Complete the following assessment.

Persuasive Essay

Ideas	Yes	No
Did I focus on one viewpoint about a specific topic?		
Does the essay work to convince the reader to share my viewpoint?		

Organization

Does the introduction include a position statement?		
Does the body include reasons and explanations?		
Does the conclusion rephrase the position statement?		

Voice

Is the voice persuasive?		
Does the voice have flair and confidence?		

Word Choice

Do I use transition words?		

Sentence Fluency

Do the sentences flow and have rhythm when put together?		

Conventions

Did I check for correct grammar?		
Did I check for correct spelling?		
Did I check for correct punctuation and capitalization?		

Name _____ Date _____

CHAPTER 6
Persuasive Essay Writing Prompt

Test items are often in the form of a prompt, a short paragraph that tells you what to write. Follow these suggestions when writing for a prompt.

1. Carefully read the prompt.
2. Circle the key words that signal the genre, in this case, a persuasive essay, and key words that signal audience or purpose.
3. Plan your writing. You might use a word web, a time line, notes, or a short outline.
4. Write a draft based on your plan.
5. Read and revise your draft.
6. Proofread and copyedit your draft.

- **Write for the following prompt. Plan your writing on this page. Write your persuasive essay on a separate sheet of paper.**

Prompt: Though you might think that your school is the best, you probably also believe that there are a few things that could be done to make your school experience even better. Choose one school improvement that you think is important to make. Write an essay for your principal that tries to persuade him or her to make the change. Be sure to include a position statement and support your ideas with reasons and explanations.

CHAPTER 7 Pre-test

- **Circle the connector in each sentence. Identify it by writing *coordinating conjunction*, *correlative conjunction*, or *conjunctive adverb*.**

1. The fair is a lot of fun(;moreover,)the food is fantastic!   **conjunctive adverb**
2. Lauren is wearing(not only)the earrings(but also)the shoes and hat.   **correlative conjunction**
3. (Both)Tanner(and)Jamie are joining us for brunch.   **correlative conjunction**
4. Ms. Jenkins lectured in Spanish(and)in English.   **coordinating conjunction**
5. We wore our raincoats(;nevertheless,)we still got soaked.   **conjunctive adverb**

- **Circle the term that correctly completes each sentence.**

6. You can bring the dog (as long as) as if) you keep him on a leash.
7. (Although) Because) the sun was shining, raindrops started to fall.
8. Tim looks (like (as if) he is very excited to play.
9. Hanna shouldn't go to the beach (without (unless) her sunscreen.
10. Staci will join us (without (unless) her class runs late.

- **Add punctuation as needed (periods, commas, semicolons, exclamation points, question marks, quotation marks, and underlining) to each sentence.**

11. I moved to Boston**,**Massachusetts**,**on August 16**,**2004**,**because my father changed jobs.
12. **"**Did you remember**,"** asked Mom**, "**to bring in the mail**?"**
13. **"**Have you seen the movie Shrek 2**?"**Brianna inquired.
14. **"**Wow**,**this is the best pizza I've ever tasted**!"** Tanya exclaimed.
15. I wanted to read Hang Time for my book report**;**however**,**my teacher assigned Where the Red Fern Grows.

- **Rewrite each sentence using periods, question marks, commas, apostrophes, hyphens, dashes, and capital letters correctly.**

16. codys youngest brother darius graduated in the class of 04
    Cody's youngest brother, Darius, graduated in the class of '04.
17. There are more seven year olds than eight year olds in ms changs class
    There are more seven-year-olds than eight-year-olds in Ms. Chang's class.
18. how many is are in the state names mississippi and illinois combined
    How many i's are in the state names Mississippi and Illinois combined?
19. myra r williams shes a good friend of mine arrived later than expected
    Myra R. Williams—she's a good friend of mine—arrived later than expected.
20. jennifer saw twenty two of Lisas relatives at saturdays concert
    Jennifer saw twenty-two of Lisa's relatives at Saturday's concert.

- **Write *true* or *false* for each statement.**

21. Dialog is the spoken words and actions of characters.   **false**
22. Dialog in plays is intended to mimic natural speech.   **true**
23. A monolog is a long section of dialog spoken by one or more people.   **false**
24. When an actor stops and addresses the audience directly, it is called a beside.   **false**

- **Draw a line to match each phrase with its meaning.**

25. have a frog in one's throat — to have a throat irritation that affects speech
26. scalpel, infarction, hypertension, saline drip — terms used by a doctor
27. turn over a new leaf — to make a new start
28. get up on the wrong side of the bed — to be in a bad mood

- **Circle the word that best completes each statement about free verse.**

29. Free verse does not follow conventional (wisdom (rules)) of rhyme and rhythm.
30. One purpose of free verse is to bring to mind certain ((emotions) jokes).
31. In free verse, the line lengths (always stay the same (may vary)).
32. The mood of a poem may be determined by the (color (rhythm)) of the language.

Name _____ Date _____

CHAPTER 7 Post-test

- **Circle the connector in each sentence. Identify it by writing *coordinating conjunction*, *correlative conjunction*, or *conjunctive adverb*.**

1. The snow was thick, (yet) I could still see the road ahead.　　**coordinating conjunction**
2. I will choose (either) the blue dress (or) the red skirt.　　**correlative conjunction**
3. The house is not finished; (consequently,) we can't move in yet.　　**conjunctive adverb**
4. Should Britney major in business (or) psychology?　　**coordinating conjunction**
5. This is (not only) the tastiest cake (but also) the prettiest dessert.　　**correlative conjunction**

- **Circle the term that correctly completes each sentence.**

6. Tamyra looks just ((like) / as) her mother.
7. ((Before) / As if) I could move, the paint fell right on my head.
8. I grabbed the books (like / (as)) the table fell over.
9. (Because / (While)) working at the library, Theo met his best friend.
10. ((Wherever) / Where) you decide to go to college, I will help you move.

- **Add punctuation as needed (periods, commas, semicolons, exclamation points, question marks, quotation marks, and underlining) to each sentence.**

11. "Please remember," reminded Mia, "to bring your textbook."
12. Has everyone read the poem "Fog" by Carl Sandburg?
13. "Yes!" Tessa shouted. "I would love to see the movie *Brother Bear*."
14. Manny is moving to Los Angeles, California, soon; moreover, he's attending college there.
15. I plan to visit the following cities: Dallas, Austin, and Houston.

- **Rewrite each sentence, using periods, question marks, commas, apostrophes, hyphens, dashes, and capital letters correctly.**

16. i laughed aloud looking back Im so embarrassed right in the middle of the speech
    Both brothers-in-law studied medicine at Stanford University in California.
17. Both brothers in law studied medicine at stanford university in california
    I laughed aloud—looking back, I'm so embarrassed—right in the middle of the speech.
18. didnt mrs capaldis ten year old son win the art contest at riverside park
    Didn't Mrs. Capaldi's ten-year-old son win the art contest at Riverside Park?
19. how many of andrea millers cats did you adopt last january
    How many of Andrea Miller's cats did you adopt last January?
20. aunt kristy gave me a watch it was very expensive for my ten year anniversary
    Aunt Kristy gave me a watch—it was very expensive—for my ten-year anniversary.

- **Write *true* or *false* for each statement.**

21. Comedies are most likely where you would hear an aside.　　**true**
22. Dialog is not influenced by the time period of a play's setting.　　**false**
23. Dialog is interesting, but it is not an important part of a play.　　**false**
24. A soliloquy is an example of a monolog.　　**true**

- **Draw a line to match each phrase with its meaning.**

25. be on a first-name basis —— regional slang
26. firewall, browser, cookie, virus —— to hurt someone who is trying to help
27. Y'all come back now, ya hear? —— to know someone well
28. bite the hand that feeds you —— terms used by a computer programmer

- **Circle the word that best completes each statement about free verse.**

29. Free verse often uses ((figurative) / irregular) language.
30. Free verse sometimes sounds like ((prose) / advertisements).
31. A whimsical mood could be created by a (slow-moving / (quick-moving)) rhythm.
32. A poem's rhythm can be measured by the number of (hands / (feet)) per line.

CHAPTER 7

Word Study: Prefixes and Suffixes

Some test items measure your ability to identify prefixes and suffixes in a word. The test item might look like this:

What is the meaning of the underlined prefix?

> I don't understand Maya's <u>anti</u>social behavior lately.

- **A** toward
- **B** between
- **C** against
- **D** many

As you read each answer choice, determine which definition matches the context of the sentences and best describes the word. Ask yourself:
What does the sentence mean?
What does the word mean in the sentence?
What is the base word? What does it mean?
What word part is added to the beginning of the base word to add to or change its meaning?
What does this beginning word part mean?

You would then choose the meaning of the prefix. In the example, you would choose answer C because

- *antisocial* can mean "hostile or harmful."
- *social* is the base word.
- *anti-* is added to *social* to change its meaning.
- it makes sense both in the word and in the sentence that *anti-* means *against*.

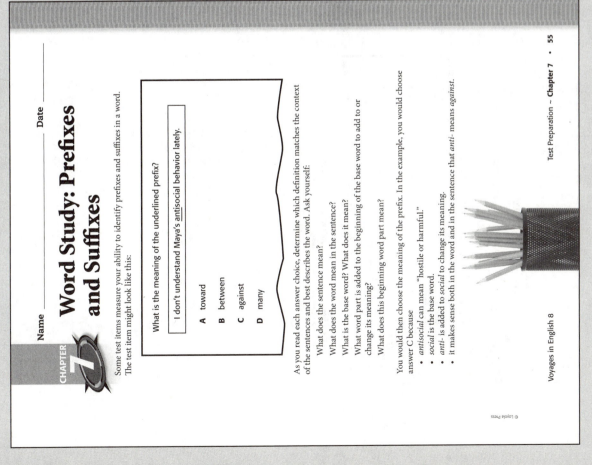

1. What is the meaning of the underlined prefix?

   > Girls <u>out</u>number boys on that soccer team.

   A again
   B toward
   C not
   D exceeding

   1. A B C **D**

2. What is the meaning of the underlined suffix?

   > The jur<u>or</u> was excused from the case.

   F the state of
   G make
   H one who does a specified thing
   J cause to be

   2. F G **H** J

3. Identify the suffix in the following word: *contentment*.

   K con
   L tent
   M ment
   N ten

   3. K L **M** N

CHAPTER 7

Playwriting Writing Prompt

Name _____ Date _____

Test items are often in the form of a prompt, a short paragraph that tells you what to write. Follow these suggestions when writing for a prompt.

1. Carefully read the prompt.
2. Circle the key words that signal the genre, in this case, a play script, and key words that signal audience or purpose.
3. Plan your writing. You might use a word web, a time line, notes, or a short outline.
4. Write a draft based on your plan.
5. Read and revise your draft.
6. Proofread and copyedit your draft.

• **Write for the following prompt. Plan your writing on this page. Write your play script on a separate sheet of paper.**

Prompt: Consider the following characters and situation. Write a one-act play that tells the story. Be sure to develop the characters and setting as you tell the story. You and your best friend get lost on a one-day hiking trip. You meet someone (a character you develop) that leads you to safety.

CHAPTER 7

Playwriting Scoring Rubric

Name _____ Date _____

• **In Chapter 7 you wrote play scripts. Read the article that you wrote for the prompt on page 57. Complete the following assessment.**

Play Script	Yes	No
Ideas		
Do I have well-developed characters?		
Do I have good plot structure?		
Organization		
Did I use standard play-script structure and format?		
Did I include a beginning that introduces a problem, conflict, or goal?		
Did I include a middle that has rising action and a climax?		
Did I include an ending that has a resolution?		
Voice		
Did I use a natural voice?		
Word Choice		
Did I choose words deliberately, such as for humor or impact?		
Sentence Fluency		
Did I use engaging, realistic dialog that moves the story along?		
Conventions		
Did I check for correct grammar?		
Did I check for correct spelling?		
Did I check for correct punctuation and capitalization?		

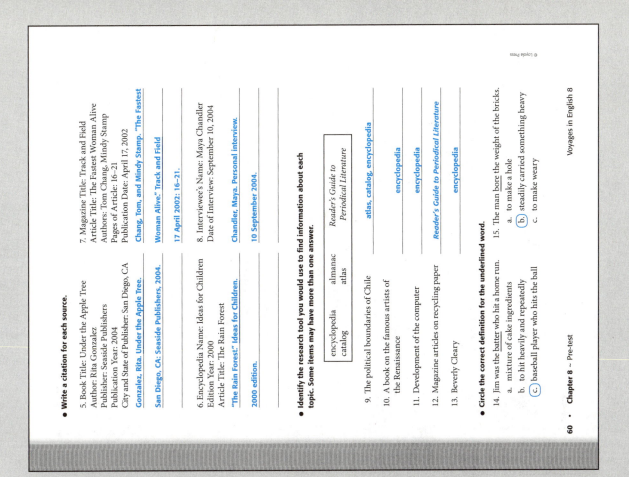

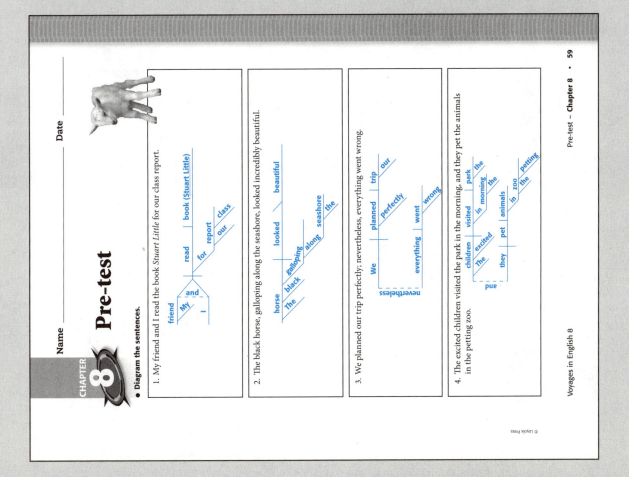

CHAPTER 8

Post-test

- **Diagram the sentences.**

1. My favorite activity, playing baseball on a cool autumn afternoon, provides the best feeling in the world.

2. Having lost my passport, I could not board the plane to take the scheduled flight.

3. Lisa and Jaime were excited to receive their final paychecks, and they rapidly completed their plans for a trip to the Greek Islands.

4. Most dedicated students will take extra classes in voice and dance after they leave acting camp.

- **Write a citation for each source.**

5. Magazine Title: Sports Unlimited
   Article Title: Baseball: America's Pastime
   Pages of Article: 9–11
   Author: Jeff Seymour
   Publication Date: March 2003

   Seymour, Jeff. "Baseball: America's Pastime."
   Sports Unlimited March 2003: 9–11.

6. Web Site Name: Recycling for Kids
   Document Title: Saving Water
   Author: Abby M. Singer
   Date Accessed: June 7, 2004
   Web Site Address: www.recycle4kids.org

   Singer, Abby M. "Saving Water." Recycling for
   Kids 7 June 2004 <www.recycle4kids.org>.

7. Newspaper Title: Boston Chronicle
   Publication Date: May 4, 2002
   Authors: Staci Walsh, Ken Weber
   Pages of Article: 12–15
   Article Title: America's Best Colleges

   Walsh, Staci, and Ken Weber. "America's Best
   Colleges." Boston Chronicle 4 May 2002: 12–15.

8. Book Title: Computer Craze
   Author: Manuel Chavez
   Publisher: TechnoPrints, Inc.
   Publication Year: 1999
   City and State of Publisher: New York, NY

   Chavez, Manuel. Computer Craze. New York,
   NY: TechnoPrints, Inc., 1999.

- **Identify the research tool you would use to find information about each topic. Some items may have more than one answer.**

| encyclopedia | almanac |
| catalog | atlas |

9. Abraham Lincoln — *encyclopedia, catalog*

10. on growing a vegetable garden — *Reader's Guide to Periodical Literature*

11. State populations over the last decade — *almanac*

12. Rivers and lakes in Montana — *atlas*

13. A book about the Pilgrims — *catalog*

- **Circle the correct definition for the underlined word.**

14. Jack ate a <u>quarter</u> of the pizza.
    a. twenty-five cents
    b. *(one-fourth)*
    c. last period in a football game

15. Please buy me a <u>pound</u> of tomatoes.
    a. to hit hard repeatedly
    b. *(a unit of weight)*
    c. English money

Name _____ Date _____

CHAPTER 8
Spelling: Irregular Spellings

Some words have irregular spellings that do not follow the standard rules. Some test items measure your ability to spell words with irregular spellings. The test item might look like this:

Which underlined word is spelled correctly?

A I used a soft shamee to dry the car.
B I used a soft chammey to dry the car.
C I used a soft chamois to dry the car.
D I used a soft shammey to dry the car.

As you read each answer choice, determine which word is spelled correctly. Ask yourself:
What does the word mean in the sentence?
What does the sentence mean?
How have I seen this word spelled before?
Which answers am I sure are wrong?
Which word looks correct, even if it is not pronounced the way it looks?

You would then choose the correct spelling. In the example, you would choose answer C because
• words like *chamois* come from languages that have different pronunciations for letters than are used in English.
• the word *chamois* looks correct.
• the words *shamee, chammey,* and *shammey* do not exist.

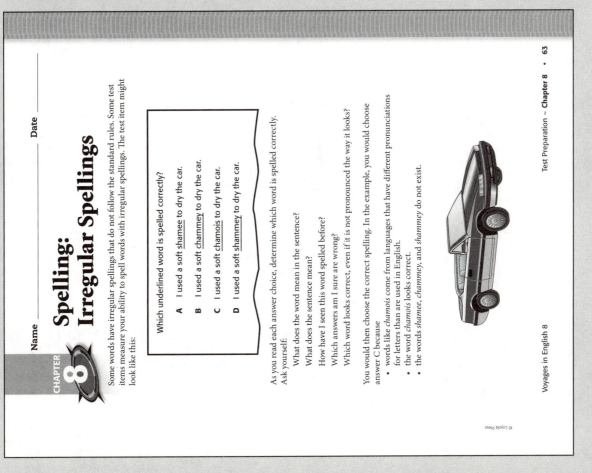

1. Which underlined word is spelled correctly?
   A My aunt has an anteek grandfather clock.
   B My aunt has an antique grandfather clock.
   C My aunt has an anteke grandfather clock.
   D My aunt has an auntique grandfather clock.

   1. A **B** C D

2. Which word best completes the following sentence?

   Hildie made me a _____ sandwich.

   F bolonie
   G balloney
   H ballonee
   J bologna

   2. F G H **J**

3. Which word best completes the following sentence?

   Sari made her singing _____ at the concert last night.

   K daybyoo
   L debut
   M daybut
   N deybuu

   3. K **L** M N

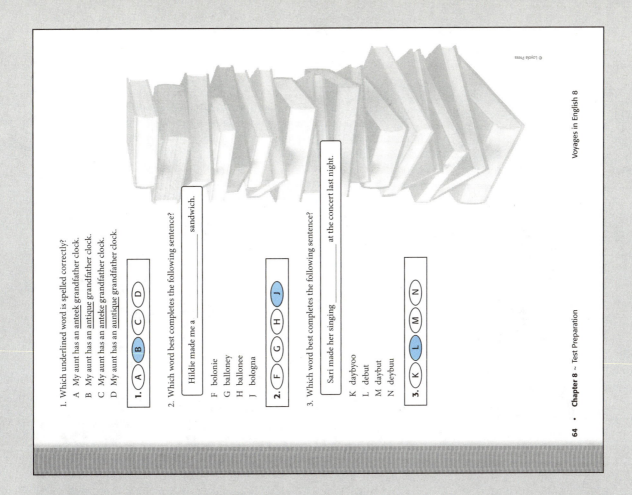

Assessment Book Answers • 107

CHAPTER 8
Research Report
Scoring Rubric

Name _____ Date _____

- In Chapter 8 you wrote research reports. Read the report that you wrote for the prompt on page 65. Complete the following assessment.

Research Report	Yes	No
Ideas		
Do I have a clear focus on one topic?		
Do I include factual information supported by research that was gathered as notes and placed in outline form?		
Organization		
Did I write an interesting introduction that includes a thesis statement?		
Did I include a body of logically ordered paragraphs that include important main ideas supported by relevant details?		
Did I write a summarizing conclusion?		
Did I include parenthetical notations and a Works Cited page?		
Voice		
Did I create a confident voice?		
Word Choice		
Did I use formal language?		
Sentence Fluency		
Did I use varied sentence styles and lengths?		
Did I vary ways of providing information, such as quotations, statistics, examples, explanations, or a related visual?		
Conventions		
Did I check for correct grammar?		
Did I check for correct spelling?		
Did I check for correct punctuation and capitalization?		

66 • Chapter 8 ~ Scoring Rubric

Voyages in English 8

CHAPTER 8
Research Report
Writing Prompt

Name _____ Date _____

Test items are often in the form of a prompt, a short paragraph that tells you what to write. Follow these suggestions when writing for a prompt.

1. Carefully read the prompt.
2. Circle the key words that signal the genre, in this case, a research report, and key words that signal audience or purpose.
3. Plan your writing. You might use a word web, a time line, notes, or a short outline.
4. Write a draft based on your plan.
5. Read and revise your draft.
6. Proofread and copyedit your draft.

- Write for the following prompt. Plan your writing on this page. Write your research report on a separate sheet of paper.

Prompt: What recent advancement in technology interests you most? Do research about this advancement. Write a research report to show what you learned.

Voyages in English 8

Writing Prompt ~ Chapter 8 • 65

108 • Voyages in English

Name _____ Date _____

Cumulative Test

- **Circle the letter of the statement that best completes each sentence.**

1. A personal narrative _____.
   a. recounts facts and statistics
   b. tells a fictional story
   c. (shares the writer's experiences)

2. When writing a personal narrative, you should pay attention to _____.
   a. rhythm and rhyme
   b. (the audience and an attention-grabbing title)
   c. fully developed characters and plot

- **Underline nouns or pronouns used as subjects once and the nouns or pronouns used as subject complements twice in each sentence.**

3. Terrance is a good speaker and has a great understanding of words.
4. Min bought exercise equipment for the team when she became coach.

- **Underline the appositive in the sentence.**

5. Tyler, my best friend, moved to New York City.

- **Rewrite the sentence to show joint possession.**

6. The kittens owned by Brent and Joy came from a shelter.
   Brent and Joy's kittens came from a shelter.

- **Circle the demonstrative adjective in the sentence. Underline the interrogative adjective.**

7. In which vase did you put (those) long-stemmed roses?

- **Circle the four activities that are organized in sequential order.**

8. (wake up, eat breakfast, leave the house, catch the bus)
   eat breakfast, wake up, catch the bus, leave the house
   leave the house, eat breakfast, catch the bus, wake up

- **Identify the sentence by writing *simple*, *compound*, or *complex* on the line.**

9. Although rain poured down on them, the football team continued to play. _____**complex**_____

- **Circle the letter of the sentence that uses the best specific, interesting adjectives.**

10. a. The dogs ran through the large park.
    b. More canned food was needed at the county homeless shelter.
    c. (Wind whispered softly through the brilliant, yellow leaves.)

- **Circle the letter of the statement that best completes each sentence.**

11. Good how-to writing includes _____.
    a. (sequence words and clear, concise steps)
    b. persuasive ideas
    c. comparing and contrasting

12. One way you can make how-to writing clearer is to _____.
    a. provide lots of descriptive details
    b. include personal experiences
    c. (get rid of unnecessary information that might distract the reader)

- **Underline the pronouns in the sentence. Then for each pronoun write its person (*first, second, third*) and number (*singular, plural*), and, where appropriate, its gender (*masculine, feminine, neuter*).**

13. Jiun and I shared our homework with him.
    I—first, singular; him—third, singular, masculine

- **Circle the subject pronoun that correctly completes the sentence.**

14. (We) Us) went to the museum to study dinosaur bones.

- **Replace the italicized words with the correct pronoun.**

15. Our soccer team won more games than *the Rockets*.   **they**

- **Rewrite the sentence so the italicized antecedent and pronoun agree.**

16. *The fuzzy caterpillar* crawls up the branch, and they seems to be looking for food.
    The fuzzy caterpillar crawls up the branch, and it seems to be looking for food.

- **Underline the indefinite pronoun in the sentence. Circle the correct verb.**

17. Everyone (is) are) excited about going on the field trip to the observatory.

- **Add punctuation and capital letters to revise this rambling sentence.**

18. Yesterday my family took a trip to the zoo and we saw many different animals including monkeys, elephants, and lions.
    Yesterday my family took a trip to the zoo. We saw many different animals, including monkeys, elephants, and lions. *or* **Yesterday my family took a trip to the zoo, where we saw many different animals—including monkeys, elephants, and lions.**

- **Read the following roots. Then choose a root to help you find a word to complete the sentence. Write the word on the line.**

    bio = life   meter = measure   arch = old   phys = body

19. The story of someone's life is called his or her _____**biography**_____.

- **Circle the pair of dictionary guidewords you would use to find the word *resplendent*.**

20. respect • respite   (respiratory • restful)   responsible • resurface

- Circle the letter of the statement that best completes each sentence.

21. The following are all parts of a business letter, except _____.
    a. heading
    (b.) phone number
    c. salutation
    d. inside address

22. In the first paragraph of a business letter, you should _____.
    a. offer relevant statistics
    b. thank the recipient for taking the requested action
    (c.) state the purpose of the letter
    d. all of the above

- Correct the italicized verb in the sentence. Write the correct verb on the first line. Then identify it by writing *simple past, past participle,* or *present participle* on the second line.

23. After the game was over, neither Alfonso nor I *know* the final score. __knew__ __simple past__

- Circle the verb in the sentence. Then identify it by writing *transitive* or *intransitive* on the line.

24. After the hike almost all of us (felt) exhausted. __intransitive__

- Rewrite the sentence in the active voice.

25. These four novels about American history were read by the entire class.
   __The entire class read these four novels about American history.__

- Underline the verb phrase in the sentence. Then write the verb phrase in past progressive and future progressive tenses.

26. Mia is writing a book about her great-grandfather.
    a. Past Progressive: __was writing__   b. Future Progressive: __will be writing__

- Circle the verb in the sentence. Then identify the mood it expresses by writing *imperative* or *indicative* on the line.

27. Please (speak) loudly and clearly during your speech. __imperative__

- Underline the adjective clause in the sentence. Then circle the noun it modifies.

28. My (sister) who lives in Italy, is coming home for the holidays.

- Write the clipped form of each word.

29. a. luncheon __lunch__   b. memorandum __memo__   c. pantaloons __pants__

- Circle the letter of the item you would *not* include on a personal check.

30. a. date   b. signature   (c.) credit card number   d. dollar amount

- Circle the letter of the statement that best completes each sentence.

31. Good descriptive writing includes _____.
    a. sensory words
    b. rhyming words
    c. precise words
    (d.) both a and c

32. All of these are good ways to organize a description, except _____.
    a. order of importance
    b. chronological
    (c.) flashback
    d. compare/contrast

- Underline the participial phrase in the sentence. Then identify it by writing *present, past,* or *perfect* on the line.

33. Jamie, having lost his backpack, could not pay for lunch. __perfect__

- Underline the gerund phrase in the sentence. Then identify it by writing *subject* or *subject complement* on the line.

34. My favorite activity is playing soccer on Saturday afternoons. __subject complement__

- Underline the gerund phrase in each sentence. Then identify it by writing *direct object, object of a preposition,* or *appositive* on the line.

35. Joaquin enjoys playing golf on Sunday afternoons. __direct object__

36. Tanya began her speech by listing statistics on rain forest destruction. __object of a preposition__

- Underline the infinitive phrase in the sentence. Then identify it by writing *adjective* or *adverb* on the line. Circle the word the infinitive phrase describes.

37. Damon's (idea) to visit all of America's baseball parks sounds exciting! __adjective__

- Circle the letter of the statement that best completes the sentence.

38. A Venn diagram helps you do all of the following, except _____.
    (a.) write information in sequential order   b. organize information
    c. compare and contrast   d. list similarities and differences

- Circle the letter of the statement that best completes the sentence.

39. You can find all of the following information in a thesaurus, except _____.
    a. synonyms   (b.) word origins
    c. antonyms   d. part of speech

- Circle the two things being compared. Then identify the comparison by writing *simile* or *metaphor* on the line.

40. (Darius) is like a (raging bull) on the football field. __simile__

Cumulative Test

- **Circle the letter of the statement that best completes each sentence.**

41. Good expository writing includes all of the following, except ____.
    a. personal opinions (circled)
    b. facts
    c. examples
    d. a clear main idea

42. Facts ____.
    a. can be proved true or false.
    b. should be credible if being used in expository writing.
    c. should be relevant to the writing topic.
    d. all of the above. (circled)

- **Write the correct positive, comparative, or superlative form of the italicized adverb on the line.**

43. Our two horses performed *beautifully* than all the others. ____more beautifully____

- **Circle the prepositions in the sentence.**

44. We picked baskets (of) apples (from) the orchard and placed them (in) the barn.

- **Circle the preposition that correctly completes the sentence.**

45. Miranda was upset (with) at) her best friend at the party.

- **Underline the prepositional phrase in each sentence. Then identify how it is used by writing *adjective, adverb,* or *noun* on the line.**

46. The box of chocolates was her favorite gift. ____adjective____
47. In the back seat is my favorite spot. ____noun____

- **Circle the letter of the item that best completes the sentence.**

48. To learn about the different branches of government, look for a URL that ends with the domain code ____.
    a. mil   b. org
    c. gov (circled)   d. edu

- **Rewrite the sentence using a noun clause. Use the word in parentheses to begin the noun clause.**

49. This manual describes the programming of your new computer. (how)
    ____This manual describes how to program your new computer.____

- **Read the group of words. Then write *before, again, one,* or *not to* identify the meaning of the underlined prefix.**

50. <u>re</u>turn, <u>re</u>read, <u>re</u>activate   ____again____

- **Circle the letter of the statement that best completes each sentence.**

51. All of the following are examples of persuasive writing, except ____.
    a. an advertisement
    b. a movie review
    c. a personal narrative (circled)
    d. a campaign speech

52. The voice or mood of a persuasive piece can be all of the following, except ____.
    a. enthusiastic
    b. concerned
    c. bored (circled)
    d. hopeful

- **Identify the sentence by writing *declarative, interrogative, imperative,* or *exclamatory* on the line.**

53. Please help me distribute these folders before class.   ____imperative____

- **Underline the adjective or adverb phrase in each sentence. On the first line identify it by writing *adjective* or *adverb*. On the second line identify it by writing *prepositional, participial,* or *infinitive*.**

54. All day, we hiked <u>to reach the mountaintop</u>.   ____adverb____   ____infinitive____
55. Several people <u>in the group</u> didn't make it all the way.   ____adjective____   ____prepositional____

- **Underline the adjective clause in the sentence. Identify it by writing *restrictive* or *nonrestrictive* on the line.**

56. Many foods <u>that we eat each day</u> are bad for our health.   ____restrictive____

- **Underline the noun clause in the sentence. Then identify it by writing *subject, subject complement, appositive, direct object,* or *object of a preposition* on the line.**

57. Shekia decided <u>that she would try out for the school play</u>.   ____direct object____

- **Identify the advertising device used in the statement by writing *bandwagon, loaded words, testimonial,* or *sweeping generalities* on the line.**

58. You won't find a better price anywhere in the state!   ____sweeping generalities____

- **Circle the transition word that best completes the sentence.**

59. I studied very hard for the test, (while (yet)) I still didn't get the grade I wanted.

- **Add the correct suffix to the italicized word to correct the sentence. Write the new word on the line.**

60. Staci is *care* with her money and blows it all on video games.   ____careless____

- Circle the letter of the statement that best completes each sentence.

61. Playwriting differs from other kinds of fiction because ___.
   a. it includes facts and figures
   b. the lines must rhyme
   (c.) it is meant to be performed

62. The features of a play include the ___.
   (a.) plot, characters, and setting
   b. characters, introduction, and closing
   c. supporting details, setting, and opinions

- Circle the correlative conjunctions in the sentence.

63. Francisco will (not only) play the trumpet (but also) lead the band in the parade.

- Circle the conjunctive adverb that correctly completes the sentence.

64. Carmen will be late for the picnic; (finally (nevertheless) we should start eating.

- Circle the conjunction that correctly completes the sentence.

65. Paolo wolfed down his food (like (as if) he hadn't eaten for weeks.

- Rewrite each sentence using correct capitalization and punctuation.

66. did you read the poem fog by carl sandburg sierra asked
   "Did you read the poem 'Fog' by Carl Sandburg?" Sierra asked.

67. mrs wyatt is the best teacher ive ever had luke told elena
   "Mrs. Wyatt is the best teacher I've ever had," Luke told Elena.

- Circle the letter of the word that best completes the sentence.

68. A long section of words spoken by only one character is a ___.
   a. dialog   b. aside   (c.) monolog

- Read the sentence. Then circle the letter of the answer that best completes the statement.

69. After a long discussion everyone in the group finally *saw eye to eye.* The italicized words in this sentence are an example of ___.
   (a.) an idiom   b. slang   c. jargon

- Write *true* or *false* to describe the statement.

70. Free verse poetry follows conventional rules of rhythm and rhyme, and the line lengths must stay the same throughout the poem.   **false**

- Circle the letter of the statement that best completes each sentence.

71. ___ should be clearly stated in the introduction of a research report.
   a. A persuasive argument
   (b.) A thesis statement
   c. A personal opinion
   d. An inside address

72. An outline for a research report should include ___.
   a. a complete introduction
   b. supporting details
   c. subtopics
   (d.) both b and c

- Diagram the sentence.

73. Our math teacher gave extra credit to whoever solved the bonus problem.

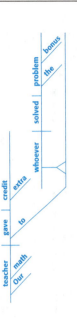

- Circle the letter of the source that is cited correctly.

74. a. Lena Jones: *Pet-Sitting Tips for the Beginner.* Chicago, IL (2004) Pet Publishers.
   b. Jones, Lena, "Pet-Sitting Tips for the Beginner" Illinois, Chicago, Pet Publishers.
   (c.) Jones, Lena. *Pet-Sitting Tips for the Beginner.* Chicago, IL: Pet Publishers, 2004.

- Circle the research tool you would use to find information about the political boundaries of North and South Korea.

75. almanac   (atlas)   biography

- Look at the italicized word in the first sentence. Circle the sentence below it in which the italicized word has the same meaning.

76. The horse began to feel restless and *strain* against its bridle.
   a. Which *strain* of flu is infecting these patients?
   (b.) The dog will *strain* at its leash, and the leash will break.
   c. Please *strain* the spaghetti with this colander.

Voyages in English
and
Exercises in English
Grammar Correlation Charts

GRADE 3

VIE Section	EIE Lesson
Sentences	
1.1	1
1.2	2
1.3	3
1.4	4
1.5	5
1.6	6
1.7	7
1.8	8
1.9	9–10
1.10	11
1.11	12
Sentence Challenge	13
Nouns	
2.1	14
2.2	15
2.3	16
2.4	17
2.5	18
2.6	19
2.7	20
2.8	21–22
2.9	23
2.10	24
2.11	25
Noun Challenge	26
Pronouns	
3.1	27–28
3.2	29
3.3	30
3.4	31
3.5	32
3.6	33
3.7	34
3.8	35–36
Pronoun Challenge	37

VIE Section	EIE Lesson
Verbs	
4.1	38–40
4.2	41
4.3	42
4.4	43
4.5	44
4.6	45–48
4.7	49–51
4.8	52–55
4.9	56
4.10	57
4.11	58
4.12	59
4.13	60
4.14	61
4.15	62
4.16	63
Verb Challenge	64
Adjectives	
5.1	65
5.2	66
5.3	67
5.4	68
5.5	69
5.6	70–71
5.7	72
5.8	73
5.9	74
5.10	75
5.11	76
Adjective Challenge	77
Adverbs and Conjunctions	
6.1	78
6.2	79
6.3	80
6.4	81–82
6.5	83
6.6	84
6.7	85
6.8	86
6.9	87
Adverb and Conjunction Challenge	88

VIE Section	EIE Lesson
Punctuation and Capitalization	
7.1	89
7.2	91–92
7.3	93–94
7.4	95
7.5	96–97
7.6	98
7.7	99
7.8	100
7.9	101
7.10	102
7.11	103–104
Punctuation and Capitalization Challenge	105
Diagramming	
8.1	106
8.2	107
8.3	108
8.4	109
8.5	110
8.6	111
8.7	112
8.8	113
8.9	114
8.10	115
Diagramming Challenge	116

VIE sections refer to 2006 edition, EIE lessons refer to 2008 edition.

GRADE 4

VIE Section	EIE Lesson
Sentences	
1.1	1
1.2	2–3
1.3	4–5
1.4	6
1.5	7–8
1.6	9
1.7	10
1.8	11
1.9	12
1.10	13
1.11	14
Sentence Challenge	15
Nouns	
2.1	16
2.2	17
2.3	18–19
2.4	20
2.5	21–22
2.6	23–24
2.7	25
2.8	26
2.9	27
2.10	28
2.11	29
Noun Challenge	30
Pronouns	
3.1	31
3.2	32–34
3.3	35
3.4	36
3.5	37
3.6	38
3.7	39
3.8	40
3.9	41
3.10	42–43
3.11	44
Pronoun Challenge	45

VIE Section	EIE Lesson
Adjectives	
4.1	46–47
4.2	48
4.3	49
4.4	50
4.5	51
4.6	52
4.7	53
4.8	54
4.9	55
4.10	56
4.11	57
Adjective Challenge	58
Verbs	
5.1	59–60
5.2	61
5.3	62
5.4	63
5.5	64
5.6	65–66
5.7	67–68
5.8	69–71
5.9	72
5.10	73
5.11	74
5.12	75–76
5.13	77
5.14	78
5.15	79
5.16	80–81
5.17	82
Verb Challenge	83

VIE Section	EIE Lesson
Adverbs and Conjunctions	
6.1	84–85
6.2	86–87
6.3	88
6.4	89
6.5	90
6.6	91
Adverb and Conjunction Challenge	92
Punctuation and Capitalization	
7.1	93–94
7.2	95
7.3	96
7.4	97
7.5	98
7.6	99–102
7.7	103–104
7.8	105
7.9	106
Punctuation and Capitalization Challenge	107
Diagramming	
8.1	108
8.2	109
8.3	110
8.4	111
8.5	112
8.6	113
8.7	114
8.8	115
8.9	116
8.10	117
Diagramming Challenge	118

VIE sections refer to 2006 edition, EIE lessons refer to 2008 edition.

GRADE 5

VIE Section	EIE Lesson
Nouns	
1.1	1–3
1.2	4
1.3	5
1.4	6–7
1.5	8
1.6	9–10
1.7	11–13
1.8	14
1.9	15
1.10	16
1.11	17–18
Noun Challenge	19
Pronouns	
2.1	20
2.2	21–22
2.3	23–25
2.4	26–27
2.5	28
2.6	29–31
2.7	32–33
2.8	34
2.9	35
2.10	36
2.11	37
Pronoun Challenge	38
Adjectives	
3.1	39
3.2	40
3.3	41
3.4	42
3.5	43
3.6	44
3.7	45
3.8	46
3.9	47
3.10	48–49
3.11	50
Adjective Challenge	51

VIE Section	EIE Lesson
Verbs	
4.1	52–55
4.2	56–57
4.3	58
4.4	59
4.5	60–64
4.6	65–66
4.7	67
4.8	68
4.9	69
4.10	70
4.11	71
Verbs Challenge	72
Adverbs	
5.1	73–76
5.2	77
5.3	78–80
5.4	81
5.5	82
Adverb Challenge	83
Prepositions, Conjunctions, Interjections	
6.1	84–87
6.2	88–89
6.3	90–92
6.4	93–97
6.5	98
6.6	99
Prepositions, Conjunctions, Interjections Challenge	100

VIE Section	EIE Lesson
Sentences	
7.1	101
7.2	102
7.3	103–105
7.4	106
7.5	107
7.6	108
7.7	109–110
7.8	111
7.9	112
7.10	113
7.11	114
Sentence Challenge	115
Punctuation and Capitalization	
8.1	116
8.2	117
8.3	118
8.4	119
8.5	120
8.6	121
8.7	122
8.8	123
8.9	124
8.10	125–126
8.11	127
Punctuation and Capitalization Challenge	128
Diagramming	
9.1	129
9.2	130
9.3	131
9.4	132
9.5	133
9.6	134
9.7	135
9.8	136
9.9	137
9.10	138
9.11	139
Diagramming Challenge	140

VIE sections refer to 2006 edition, EIE lessons refer to 2008 edition.

GRADE 6

VIE Section	EIE Lesson
Nouns	
1.1	1
1.2	2
1.3	3
1.4	4
1.5	5–6
1.6	7–9
1.7	10–11
1.8	12
1.9	13–14
1.10	15
1.11	16
Noun Challenge	17
Pronouns	
2.1	18–19
2.2	20
2.3	21
2.4	22–23
2.5	24–26
2.6	27–29
2.7	30
2.8	31
2.9	32
2.10	33–34
2.11	35
Pronoun Challenge	36
Adjectives	
3.1	37–38
3.2	39
3.3	40
3.4	41–42
3.5	43
3.6	44
3.7	45
3.8	46–47
3.9	48
3.10	49
3.11	50
Adjective Challenge	51

VIE Section	EIE Lesson
Verbs	
4.1	52–53
4.2	54
4.3	55–56
4.4	57
4.5	58–59
4.6	60–61
4.7	62
4.8	63
4.9	64–66
4.10	67–73
4.11	74
4.12	75
4.13	76
4.14	77
4.15	78
4.16	79
Verb Challenge	80
Adverbs	
5.1	81–83
5.2	84–85
5.3	86–87
5.4	88
5.5	89
5.6	90
Adverb Challenge	91
Parts of Sentences	
6.1	92–94
6.2	95–96
6.3	97–99
6.4	100–101
6.5	102–103
6.6	104–105
6.7	106–107
6.8	108
6.9	109–110
6.10	111–112
6.11	113
Sentence Challenge	114

VIE Section	EIE Lesson
Conjunctions, Interjections, Punctuation, Capitalization	
7.1	115–118
7.2	119–121
7.3	122
7.4	123–127
7.5	128
7.6	129
7.7	130
7.8	131
7.9	132
7.10	133
7.11	134
Conjunction, Interjection, Punctuation, Capitalization Challenge	135
Diagramming	
8.1	136
8.2	137
8.3	138
8.4	139
8.5	140
8.6	141
8.7	142
8.8	143
8.9	144
8.10	145
Diagramming Challenge	146

VIE sections refer to 2006 edition, EIE lessons refer to 2008 edition.

GRADE 7

VIE Section	EIE Lesson
Nouns	
1.1	1–2
1.2	3
1.3	4
1.4	4–7
1.5	8–9
1.6	10–12
Noun Challenge	13
Adjectives	
2.1	14–15
2.2	16–17
2.3	18–19
2.4	20–21
2.5	22–23
Adjective Challenge	24
Pronouns	
3.1	25–26
3.2	27–28
3.3	29–31
3.4	32
3.5	33
3.6	34
3.7	35
3.8	36–37
3.9	28
3.10	39
3.11	40
Pronoun Challenge	41
Verbs	
4.1	42–44
4.2	45–46
4.3	47
4.4	48–49
4.5	50
4.6	51–53
4.7	54–55
4.8	56
4.9	57
4.10	58–61
4.11	62–66
Verb Challenge	67

VIE Section	EIE Lesson
Verbals	
5.1	68
5.2	69–70
5.3	71–72
5.4	73–74
5.5	75
5.6	76
5.7	77
5.8	78
5.9	79
5.10	80
5.11	81
Verbal Challenge	82
Adverbs	
6.1	83
6.2	84–85
6.3	86
6.4	87–90
6.5	91–92
Adverb Challenge	93
Prepositions	
7.1	94–95
7.2	96–97
7.3	98
7.4	99
7.5	100
7.6	101
Preposition Challenge	102
Phrases, Clauses, Sentences	
8.1	103–106
8.2	107
8.3	108
8.4	109–110
8.5	111–112
8.6	113
8.7	114
8..8	115
8.9	116
8.10	117
8.11	118–122
Phrases, Clauses, Sentences Challenge	123

VIE Section	EIE Lesson
Conjunctions, Interjections	
9.1	124
9.2	125
9.3	126
9.4	127
9.5	128
9.6	129
Conjunctions, Interjections Challenge	130
Punctuation and Capitalization	
10.1	131–135
10.2	136–137
10.3	138
10.4	139
10.5	140
Punctuation and Capitalization Challenge	141
Diagramming	
11.1	142
11.2	143
11.3	144
11.4	145
11.5	146
11.6	147
11.7	148
11.8	149
11.9	150
11.10	151
Diagramming Challenge	152

VIE sections refer to 2006 edition, EIE lessons refer to 2008 edition.

GRADE 8

VIE Section	EIE Lesson
Nouns	
1.1	1
1.2	2
1.3	3
1.4	4–5
1.5	6
1.6	7–8
Noun Challenge	9
Adjectives	
2.1	10–11
2.2	12
2.3	13–14
2.4	15
2.5	16–17
Adjective Challenge	18
Pronouns	
3.1	19–20
3.2	21–22
3.3	22–24
3.4	25
3.5	26
3.6	27–28
3.7	29
3.8	30–33
3.9	33–34
3.10	35
3.11	36
Pronoun Challenge	37
Verbs	
4.1	38
4.2	39
4.3	40
4.4	41
4.5	42
4.6	43–45
4.7	46
4.8	47
4.9	48
4.10	49–51
4.11	52–57
Verb Challenge	58

VIE Section	EIE Lesson
Verbals	
5.1	59
5.2	60–61
5.3	62–63
5.4	64–66
5.5	67–68
5.6	69–70
5.7	71–72
5.8	73
5.9	74
5.10	75
5.11	76–77
Verbal Challenge	78
Adverbs	
6.1	79
6.2	80–81
6.3	82
6.4	83
6.5	84
Adverb Challenge	85
Prepositions	
7.1	86
7.2	87
7.3	88
7.4	89
7.5	90
7.6	91
Preposition Challenge	92
Sentences, Phrases, Clauses	
8.1	93–101
8.2	102
8.3	103–104
8.4	105
8.5	106–108
8.6	109
8.7	110
8.8	111
8.9	112
8.10	113–115
8.11	116–119
Sentences, Phrases, Clauses Challenge	120

VIE Section	EIE Lesson
Conjunctions, Interjections	
9.1	121
9.2	122
9.3	123
9.4	124
9.5	125
9.6	126
Conjunction, Interjection Challenge	127
Punctuation and Capitalization	
10.1	128–132
10.2	133–134
10.3	135
10.4	136
10.5	137
Punctuation and Capitalization Challenge	138
Diagramming	
11.1	139
11.2	140
11.3	141
11.4	142
11.5	143
11.6	144
11.7	145
11.8	146
11.9	147
11.10	148
Diagramming Challenge	149

VIE sections refer to 2006 edition, EIE lessons refer to 2008 edition.